I0085707

Carausius

A consideration of the historical, archaeological and numismatic aspects of his reign

Hugh P.G.Williams

BAR British Series 378

2004

Published in 2016 by
BAR Publishing, Oxford

BAR British Series 378

Carausius

ISBN 978 1 84171 656 5

© H P G Williams and the Publisher 2004

The author's moral rights under the 1988 UK Copyright,
Designs and Patents Act are hereby expressly asserted.

All rights reserved. No part of this work may be copied, reproduced, stored,
sold, distributed, scanned, saved in any form of digital format or transmitted
in any form digitally, without the written permission of the Publisher.

BAR Publishing is the trading name of British Archaeological Reports (Oxford) Ltd.
British Archaeological Reports was first incorporated in 1974 to publish the BAR
Series, International and British. In 1992 Hadrian Books Ltd became part of the BAR
group. This volume was originally published by Archaeopress in conjunction with
British Archaeological Reports (Oxford) Ltd / Hadrian Books Ltd, the Series principal
publisher, in 2004. This present volume is published by BAR Publishing, 2016.

Printed in England

BAR
PUBLISHING

BAR titles are available from:

BAR Publishing
122 Banbury Rd, Oxford, OX2 7BP, UK
EMAIL   info@barpublishing.com
PHONE   +44 (0)1865 310431
FAX   +44 (0)1865 316916
www.barpublishing.com

Contents

Abstract

This study relates the significant bronze coinage of the usurper Carausius, 286-93, to the archaeological and historical evidence from the period. Since the publication of Roman Imperial Coinage. Volume V(ii) in 1933, many new and significant coin types have appeared. Several important hoards have been published in the intervening years which throw a new light on discussions of the chronology of the coinage, enabling a modified sequence of issues to be postulated. Part of an important hoard discovered in the 1980's has been reconstituted. Much information regarding the archaeology of Roman Britain in the latter half of the third century has been published during the last three decades, and this is discussed in conjunction with the coin evidence of site finds.

Consideration is made of the probable methods employed in the striking of the coinage, and a new mathematical method is invoked to yield a more accurate picture of the supply of coinage under the Carausian administration. A study of the metrology of the bronze coinage is made and this includes the illustration of the metrology with a three-dimensional surface using computer graphics.

Consideration of the geographical distribution of the index-marked coinage has enabled a new interpretation of the location of the minting centres to be forwarded.

The older historical sources have been reconsidered and important new interpretations have been made. Certain aspects of the coinage which relate to the history have been examined in the light of newly discovered coin types.

The study involved the examination of approximately seven thousand specimens of the coinage from both public and private collections and excavations.

Acknowledgements

I have received support from numerous members of the numismatic fraternity during the execution of this research project. Above all I thank Professor Michael Fulford for his continued advice and support throughout the whole period of research and writing. I would also like to thank Dr. Roger Bland and Dr. Andrew Burnett of the British Museum and Dr. Cathy King of the Ashmolean Museum, Oxford for their patience in dealing with all of my enquiries. Dr. Bland also provided me with some working photographs of specimens in the British Museum, and Dr. King provided me with details and photographs of coins from the excavations at Corinium in addition to giving me the opportunity to examine the Carausian element of an important and as yet unpublished hoard from Dorchester.

I would like to thank Dr. David Sellwood for conversations about ancient minting techniques, and for his encouragement and perpetual good humour. Dr. Richard Reece and Mr. John Casey are thanked for providing me with much useful information and coin lists from several important excavations. I thank Ms. Jude Plouviez for informing me of the hoard of Carausian coins discovered at Baylham in Suffolk, and for arranging for me an opportunity to inspect and record its contents. Dr. Edward Besly provided me with opportunity to view several unpublished accumulations at the National Museum of Wales, and Mr. Graham Dyer made it possible for me to study the collection in the museum of the Royal Mint. Dr. Keith Sugden provided me with details and photographs of the Carausian coins in Manchester Museum. My thanks are also recorded to all other museum keepers that have kindly arranged for me to study the collections in their care.

I must record my thanks to many members of the coin trade who, being aware of the nature of my project, have kept me informed of unpublished material passing through their trays, my special appreciation goes to Mr. Thomas Curtis, Mr. Alan Cherry and Mr. David Miller. Mr. Andrew Barrett deserves special credit for bringing the lead sealing of Carausius to my attention.

A number of private collectors have kindly made important collections available to me for study, this has enabled me to record many unpublished types, some of which have important implications referred to in this study. Much as I would like to name them here, I feel it only right that their anonymity is respected but nevertheless thank them sincerely for all their help.

Finally I wish to thank my family for enduring the foibles of a full-time schoolmaster and a part-time research student over the past few years.

I dedicate this work to the memory of my father, Dr. Gordon Williams (1916-91). Without his encouragement and financial support in its early years, this project would have not been possible.

List of figures

Chapter One

Introduction

The study of the so called 'First British Empire' has, over the years, held a special fascination for the inhabitants of this island. The basic story of the breakaway from Roman authority and subsequent setting up of an ostensibly independent regime executed by Carausius, commander of the Channel Fleet, is well recorded in ancient sources.

In more modern times interest was rekindled by the works of two eighteenth century antiquaries Stukeley and Genebrier who both produced works dealing in some detail, though often without any sound evidence, with the life and times of the Emperor (Genebrier 1740 and Stukeley 1757, illustrated overleaf). The latter work was almost entirely based on a study of the only tangible evidence of the reign that remains in any quantity, namely the coinage, but unfortunately much of the work remains a product of Stukeley's over-fertile imagination and its contents, though sometimes amusing, cannot be treated with any credibility.

More rigorous attempts to analyse the numismatic evidence were made in the nineteenth century (Akerman 1834 and Cohen 1885), but the first work to combine a full study of the known coinage with summary of the historical works came in 1907 with the publication in the Numismatic Chronicle by Percy Webb of 'The Reign and Coinage of Carausius, 287-93 (Webb 1907). This work contained a comprehensive listing of all known coin varieties and provided the basis for the Carausian section published in Roman Imperial Coinage, Volume V(ii) (Webb 1933), which, for over fifty years, has remained the standard reference work on the subject. Since the publication of this volume many other coin-types have come to light, especially during the last decade with the advent of the metal detector. The purpose of this work is not to supersede the revision of R.I.C. by producing any listing of such coins but to consider the coinage as a whole, focussing only on certain aspects, in order to create an overview of the numismatic content from the reign and its relationship to the historical and archaeological evidence.

In 1977, Shiel published The Episode of Carausius and Allectus which gave emphasis to the gold and silver coinage of the breakaway empire, and in 1984 the British Numismatic Society organised a colloquium on the subject which led to the publication of several important papers in the British Numismatic Journal (1984). In 1994, Casey published Carausius and Allectus, the British Usurpers, which looks in general terms at aspects of the two reigns.

The last forty years have witnessed the publication of many papers devoted to Carausian numismatics. This period has also seen the publication of many works dealing with the archaeology of Roman Britain relating to the second half of the third century. A purpose of this study is to combine both these areas of research.

The contents of this project can briefly be outlined as follows. Though the works of the panegyrists writing, albeit from a slightly biased viewpoint, give a contemporary view of certain events which have been considered by many previous students there remains in such works a certain amount of room for re-interpretation. The wording of such works is, by the very laudatory nature of their content, often punctuated with fairly obscure allusions to events. As such the contents should be studied and any possible reinterpretation of any major point should be discussed.

The work of later Roman historians also requires some discussion. Though the extant accounts of the reign of Carausius date from some decades after his usurpation, they form, nevertheless, a valuable source of information. Much discussion has taken place in modern times relating to the actual dates of the main events of the reign, and some insight into this chronology should be found in these works.

The English chroniclers Bede, Nennius and Geoffrey of Monmouth seem to add little to the works previously considered. The content of all has been well studied over many years and as such their writings are deemed unlikely to add any fresh information to this study. The works of two medieval Scottish historians, John Fordun and Hector Boethius are, however, included. Writing in the fourteenth and fifteenth centuries respectively, their works contain elements of folklore and many inaccuracies but even so should not be dismissed out of hand. Much of what they report agrees with the earlier works and is of a reasonable degree of accuracy and bearing this in mind a study has been made of the contents of these often neglected works. Though many of the ideas presented are obviously invented to embellish the story and to give it a nationalistic flavour, there are otherwise unrecorded events described which may contain elements of truth possibly passed down in local folklore over the intervening centuries.

A discussion of the archeology of third century Britain forms a major part of this study. Though, by its very nature, such evidence is rarely capable of precise dating, evidence of constructional or demolition activities on sites throughout the province must play a large part in

THE

MEDALLIC HISTORY

OF

MARCVS AVRELIVS VALERIVS
CARAVSIVS,

EMPEROR in *BRITTAIN*.

———————————

BOOK I.

———————————

By *WILLIAM STUKELEY*, M.D.

Rector of St. George, Queen-Square, *Fellow of the* COLLEGE *of*
PHYSICIANS, *of the* ROYAL *and* ANTIQUARIAN SOCIETYS.

═══════════════

LONDON:

Printed for CHARLES CORBET, Bookseller, over-against
St. *Dunstan's-Church, Fleet-Street.*

———————————

M.DCC.LVII.

Frontispeice

W. *Stukeley delin. ex numismate argenteo ampliato,*
penes Matt. Duane Ar. maij 22. 1756.

FIGURE 1   TITLE PAGE AND FRONTISPIECE OF STUKELEY'S WORK, 1757

any discussion of the events of the last two decades of the century. Much information yielded by excavation has been published in recent years and an effort needs to be made to link this evidence for population deployment to the distribution of Carausian coinage found on British sites. Several areas are of prime importance if we are to gain a sound understanding of the mechanics of the Carausian regime. A consideration needs to be made of activity in the area of Hadrian's Wall, and also of the part played by the forts of the mis-named Saxon Shore. Changes in activity in the townships needs to be looked at, as does the apparent increase in activity on several sites in Wales.

Any general study of the coinage should commence with a discussion of both the size of the coinage and its method of production. A study of the metrology of any coinage is likely to produce someuseful information, though the bronze coinage of Carausius is of variable standard.

Attempts have been made by using the coins from excavations to calculate the relative coin supply to Britain in different periods. Ravetz (Ravetz 1963) proposed a method which simply depended on the length of the period of issue of a particular coinage and its relative abundance on the site in question. Though the employment of such a method is reasonable in some instances, in the case of Carausius and Allectus there are certain inherent failings that are likely to give most misleading results. Such a problem is complicated by the fact that it is unlikely that a high percentage of such coins would form casual losses on these sites, since their circulation lifetime would be curtailed by the recoinage that immediately followed the reconquest of Britain by Constantius 296 (Eichholz 1953). A new and much more detailed mathematical approach has to be invoked, necessitating the setting up and subsequent solution of differential equations, if a true indication of relative supply rates is to be forthcoming.

The chronology of any coinage is one of its most important features. The Carausian coinage seems to have been produced at several minting centres, and it exhibits a wide selection of index-marks which should fit into a logical pattern, from which the sequence of issues may be determined. Possible sequences have been put forward by Webb (Webb 1933) and Carson (Carson 1959 and 1971). Such schemes may be put together by using hoard evidence and stylistic considerations, the latter by its very nature being subjective. In the light of recent hoard evidence those systems referred to above now need considerable re-appraisal and this work will put forward a modified chronology of the coinage of Carausius.

The geographical location of the minting centres used by Carausius has, for many years, been a contentious issue in the study of Romano-British numismatics. The more common markings on the bronze coinage contain an L or a C, though many coins carry no marks at all. There are also rarer marks such as RSR and BRI that need some consideration. For many years the L coins have been attributed to Londinium whist the C coins have been attributed to several places, the most commonly accepted being either Camulodunum or Clausentum. This study will look at the geographical distribution of coins bearing the different index-marks and consider the various suggestions for the location of these minting centres.

The numismatic evidence provided by hoards is of major importance. Though Shiel (Shiel ibid) gives a comprehensive listing of hoards, many of those referred to were discovered in the nineteenth century and are poorly documented. As such much of the information tendered is unreliable. In this work only well documented hoards are considered together with those important hoards published since Shiel's work. Also considered is the Carausian element of a recent hoard from Dorchester (King forthcoming) and a Carausian hoard from Baylham in Suffolk (Williams forthcoming). In the late 1980's a large Carausian hoard was discovered and sold in trade before a detailed examination was possible. This hoard is henceforth referred to as the '1987' Hoard and is discussed in some detail. An attempt is made in this work to reconstitute a small part of this hoard.

Several aspects of the coinage itself are worthy of new scrutiny. A rare group of coins bear legends which cite tribunal or consular powers, and although such titles would have been granted without the sanction of Rome, and awarded by Carausius to himself, they nevertheless would have played an important part in the propaganda conveyed by the coinage and as such they would be expected to conform to a logical pattern which hitherto has not been well explained. Members of the emperor's family are often alluded to on the Roman Imperial coinage. Although the existence of Oriuna, forwarded by Stukeley as the wife of Carausius, has long been regarded as mythical, there do exist certain coins which may refer in some way to the family of the Emperor. These are examined in some detail. Carausius issued coinage commemorating several legions, some of whom are unknown in a British context. These have formed a basis for discussion (Oman 1924) but in the light of modern evidence need re-assessment. A final aspect worthy of consideration is a study of the relative abundance of the PAX reverse type, so common that it constitutes over half the bronze issues of Carausius. At no other time in the whole imperial series does one reverse type so dominate such a large and varied collection of known reverse types.

This study has involved the personal examination and recording of approximately seven thousand specimens of the coinage of Carausius, of which all but a mere handful were bronze antoniniani. Where possible the mass (the term 'mass' is used throughout this work rather than 'weight' as the latter is scientifically incorrect) and diameter of each coin together with the epigraphic and design details was recorded and a large number were also photographed. Masses were registered on a small portable Ohaus balance which registered to ñ0.01 grams, and diameters were measured with a vernier callipers. Photographs were taken with a Zenit E SLR camera fitted with extension rings and mounted on a specially made copying stand. In all but a very few cases colour photographs were taken, and these have been used in the production of the plates reproduced in this work. Colour photographs provided a much better working platform than monochrome photographs, since the effects of corrosion were much more clearly displayed on the images reducing the risk of misreading small details. This having been said, it must be pointed out that with the exception of a few special issues, the bronze coinage of Carausius is particularly unphotogenic.

The coins examined came from four major sources: public collections housed in museums, excavation coins in the possession of various archaeological units, coins passing through the trade and viewed in the trays of coin dealers who have generally been most helpful in assisting this research, and finally a large number of coins in private collections that the owners have kindly made available for my studies.

The public collections visited include the following:
The British Museum, London
The Bibliothèque Nationale, Paris
The Ashmolean Museum, Oxford
The National Museum of Wales, Cardiff
The Fitzwilliam Museum, Cambridge
Verulamium Museum
Corinium Museum, Cirencester
Hereford Museum
Museum of London
Lincoln Museum
Colchester Museum
Reading Museum
Leeds City Museum
Nottingham University Museum
 Newport Museum
Shrewsbury Museum
Carmarthen Museum
Exeter Museum
Chichester Museum
Andover Museum
Winchester Museum
Portsmouth Museum
The Yorkshire Museum, York
Guildford Museum
Swindon Museum
Devizes Museum
Taunton Museum
Bristol City Museum
Chester Museum
Salisbury Museum

HUGH P.G.WILLIAMS

Bath Museum
Farnham Museum
Oxford County Museum, Woodstock
The Royal Mint Museum, Llantrissant
Hampshire County Museums Collection

(Details and photographs of Carausian coins in Manchester Museum were kindly supplied to me by Dr.K.Sugden)

Excavation coins studied included those held by HBMC in London (coins from Richborough and Aldborough),

Suffolk Archaeological Unit, Lincoln Archaeological Trust, and the Department of Archaeology at the University of Durham.

(Details and photographs of Carausian coins from recent excavations at Corinium were kindly supplied by Dr. C. E. King)

It is the hope of the author that the content of this work will improve our understanding of this short period of history.

Chapter Two

The Historical Evidence

Britain at the End of the Third Century

The assassination of Gordian III in 244 opened a period of turmoil in the Roman World, with a long succession of Military Commanders seizing and losing power with the aid of legions under their command. Against this troubled backdrop, however, Britain seems to have avoided almost all the upheavals that accompany such violent and bloody revolts. The English Channel had provided a barrier to the south, and all indications suggest that the Northern Frontier was now in a state of peace. There is little evidence of military activity within the province after the campaigns of Septimius Severus in 208-211. Some building is known to have taken place on both the Northern Frontier, and at the Legionary Fortress in Chester (Frere 1967), under Severus Alexander, 222-235, but the years that follow yield a distinct lack of any contemporary epigraphic evidence. When Postumus set up the break-away Gallic Empire in 259, comprising of Gaul and Spain, it is clear that the Province of Britannia gave him every support.

Economically, the second half of the third century was a time of acute inflation. The antoninianus had been debased from a coin of approximately 50% silver at its introduction in 214 (Cope 1974), to a much smaller coin devoid of any significant silver content by the end of the Gallic Empire in 273.

The observation that many of the larger hoards found in Britain terminate with the Tetrici may well be due, as Frere indicates (Frere ibid), to the fact that the 270's saw an increase in the raiding activities of the Saxon pirates. To attribute this trend to this one tenuous factor does, undoubtedly, oversimplify the matter. There are no epigraphic accounts of raiding at this time, and there remains uncertainty as to the ability of these pirates to successfully navigate regular cross-channel raids (Cotterill 1993).

The return to Central Empire was not accompanied by the expected bloodshed, but merely involved the submission of Tetricus and his son to Aurelian, their lives being spared, and a good sinecure being provided. Thus, once again, Britannia escaped the ravages of internal strife, although the uncertainty of the situation may well have led, in some part, to the concealment of a significant number of hoards.

The relative worthlessness of the coins themselves is an important factor in explaining the size of the hoards. Any personal deposit having the significant value to require burying would amount to a large number of coins, and many smaller hoards may never have been recovered as the rampant inflation would have made such an exercise unrewarding.

The only possibility of the tranquillity of the province being disturbed is mentioned by Frere (Frere ibid). He puts forward the possibility that the Governor of Britain may have rebelled about 280, but that the revolt was quickly quelled by an army that now contained a significant Barbarian element of Burgundian and Vandallic irregulars.

Thus the years prior to the Carausian revolt would, in all probability, have constituted a time of relative peace and plenty reflected on the UBERITAS denarius (Plate 2, Nos.14-15), showing a milk-maid with a full-uddered cow in a scene of rural tranquillity, though the Vergilian connotations sometimes suggested for this type (Casey 1994) are somewhat tentative.

The Carlisle Milestone

Contemporary epigraphic evidence of the reign of Carausius is limited to a single inscription (R.I.B.2291) on a milestone found on the bed of the River Peterill near Carlisle in 1894 (Haverfield 1895). The stone is almost two metres high, and is now housed in Carlisle Museum (Plate 1).

The inscription reads

IMPCM
AVRMAVS
CARAVSIOPF
INVICTO AVG

The milestone was only used for a short period of time before being turned upside down and re-engraved thus

FLVAL
CONSTANT (...)
ONOB
CAES

The nature of the missing letter of letters is of great significance in the attribution of this re-engraving. The stone could either read *CONSTANTIO*, and refer to Constantius I, who was *Caesar* from 293 to 305, or alternatively it could read *CONSTANTINO* and refer to the brief Caesarship of Constantine I which would date the inscription to 305-6.

Haverfield (*ibid*) believed that there was sufficient room for two letters, and favoured the latter reading. In support of his argument he cites two other inscriptions belonging to Constantine I as having been found on the road South from Carlisle.

The arguments in favour of the stone originally reading *CONSTANTIO*, and referring to Constantius as *Caesar*, are, however, much stronger. Breeze (Breeze 1982) refers to activity on the Wall shortly after the reconquest of *Britannia* undertaken by Constantius in 296. It is reasonable to suppose that the name of Carausius would be *damnatio* in the eyes of the restored regime, and that any milestone bearing such an inscription would have been replaced without delay.

The milestone does, however, yield information on two important points. Firstly it gives direct evidence of the authority of Carausius reaching the far North-West of the province. The implication of this fact on some of the claims made by the Scottish chronicler Hector Boethius is discussed later.

Secondly, the inscription gives an indication of a third *praenomen* used by Carausius. It has been suggested that *MAVS* may well be an abbreviated form of Mausaeus or a similar Romano-Celtic name (Webb 1907). Coins do exist with the obverse legend *IMP C M AV M CARAVSIVS P F AVG*, R.I.C.365 and 369, re-enforcing the likelihood of a name beginning with *M*. Both these coins bear the reverse legend *PROVID AVGGG*, and carry the index-mark *S/P/C*, dating them to the latter half of the reign. If the milestone engraving is contemporary with these two coins, then it is likely to belong to the period 291-3.

Haverfield (*ibid*) was prepared to cast some doubt on such an unusual *praenomen* and accepted that the lettering possibly incorporated an engraver's error for *MAVR*. Such caution is required in this instance, especially in view of the "eccentric orthography on other third century British milestones" (Birley 1981).

The Panegyrists

The only contemporary literary evidence that remains extant comes from two panegyrics. The former was in all probability delivered to Maximian at Treveri in 289 at the outset of his attempt to defeat Carausius and retake Britain. This panegyric has been attributed to Claudius Mamertinus (Webb 1907). All the translations quoted below are also taken from Webb's work.

All panegyrics, by their very nature, give a biased view of events. Nevertheless, much can be read between the lines, and some otherwise lost information may be gleaned from their contents.

This first panegyric refers to the enormity of the task of constructing a fleet large enough to challenge the naval supremacy of Carausius, and even gives us an insight into the mild weather experienced that winter, followed by heavy spring rains. "*Throughout almost a whole year ,Emperor, during which you had need of fine weather to construct your dockyards,........ scarcely a day was spoiled by rain. Even winter resembled spring in mildness, and we did not think that we lay under the northern sky,......but felt that we were enjoying the clemency of a southern clime. Suddenly when the galleys had to be launched ,Earth for you sent up abundant springs, and Jupiter for you poured down copious rains.*" The most important and enigmatic passage in the panegyric, however, refers to some form of skirmishing, at the very least, on the mainland of the continent."*Your soldiers have reached the ocean victorious, and already the ebb and flow of the tide have sucked in the blood of your enemies slain upon that coast.*" This must indicate that a Carausian foothold on the continent was removed, with some bloodshed before early 289. Casey (Burnett and Casey 1984), supports this idea stating that there could be no context for such a claim in the panegyric if Carausius had not held any continental territory before 289. This does not challenge the view that Carausius assumed the purple whilst based on the continent,before his landing in Britain. The issue of the Rouen mint can now, on hoard evidence from Normanby (Bland and Burnett 1988), Croydon (Burnett 1985) and Dorchester (King forthcoming), be firmly attributed to the beginning of the reign. If Carausius had declared himself emperor at Rouen, it seems quite likely that he would have maintained a garrison in that city, even after his main power base had been relocated to Britain. It thus seems quite possible that the remaining troops were defeated and slain upon that coast sometime during 287.

The expedition of 289 ended in failure for Maximian. If credence is placed on the latter panegyric, then the disaster may have been due to a storm at sea, an ironic twist of fate in the light of the emphasis placed by Maximian's panegyrist on the good will of the gods in providing favourable weather. Although the weather may indeed have played some part in the downfall of the expedition, it is also extremely likely that the Carausian naval power and the expertise of his officers, so skilled in maritime manoeuvres, was the major factor, and that Maximian's fleet was destroyed in battle somewhere in the channel.

This supposition is supported by the later Roman historians who mention a peace, reflected on the coinage (Plate 2 No.5), drawn up between Carausius, Maximian and Diocletian. A naval victory being much more likely to have given Carausius a negotiating platform than a channel storm.

The second panegyric, usually ascribed to Eumenius, gives a description of some of the events from 292-296, though the chronological order is not always clear, and as expected the overall emphasis tendered is pro-Constantius, and probably "economical with the truth" in certain aspects. This panegyric is believed to have been delivered on the first of March 297, that date being the fourth anniversary of the elevation of Constantius to the rank of Caesar (Shiel 1977). By this time Britain had been successfully recovered, and the panegyric deals in a fairly detailed way with the final victory of Constantius over Allectus.

The panegyric does, however, enable us to piece together some information relating to the latter months of the reign of Carausius. The dating of the commencement of Constantius's siege of Boulogne is accurately defined by its contents. " *Adopted into the supreme power, immediately upon his arrival, he shut out the ocean seething with a fleet of enemies beyond all count, and hemmed in by sea that army which had settled on the Boulogne shore.*"

Constantius was elevated to the title Caesar on 1st March 293 (Shiel *ibid)*, thus the passage indicates that a foothold on the continent at Boulogne had already been established by this time. It records that one of the first moves of the new Caesar was to set up the extraordinary siege of Boulogne, described in much detail in the panegyric. The panegyric continues..." *And he, having conquered by his valour the army of Carausius, and in his mercy saving it...*"

This accurately dated defeat of the Boulogne based army has generally been assumed to be one of the final acts of the Carausian regime, and has often been cited as possibly the excuse that Allectus needed to succeed in his coup. There is, however, another possibility brought to light by a statement in chap.xii of the panegyric, which has not yet been fully explored. It refers to the assassination of Carausius in the following way, *"The henchman slew the arch-pirate, and thought that the Empire was a fit reward for such a crime."*

There is little doubt over the identities of the characters concerned, but the final comment about the Empire being the reward for the crime of the assassination, makes a new interpretation possible. The passage may convey the information that it was Allectus who landed troops on the continental shore in the hope of increasing his share of the empire to include at least part of Gaul.

There is little doubt over the military skill exercised by Carausius during his reign, and in many ways it would seem unlikely that he would risk a foolish sortie from his hitherto impregnable island stronghold. The possibility must therefore exist that Carausius was removed from power by an ambitious expansionist who immediately deployed, perhaps over-eager, troops to gain a continental foothold at Boulogne. The later historians speak of the peace negotiated by Carausius with Maximian, and there would seem little point in Carausius destroying this somewhat advantageous *status quo*.

Against this argument may be raised the point that the panegyric refers to the capture of the Carausian, rather than Allectan army at Boulogne. The army captured would, however, have been that assembled and trained under Carausius, and it would possibly be advantageous in such a laudatory address to ascribe the defeated forces to a general grudgingly accepted by the central empire as being both skilful and courageous.

Before giving a vivid description of the retaking of Britain and Constantius's subsequent arrival in an anarchic London, the panegyrist does make mention of the failed expedition of 289, referring to "......*the storminess of the sea, which, by a fatal necessity had deferred our victory* " .Whether the tempest was the only or the main factor in the failure of Maximian's initial attempt remains open to conjecture.

The Later Roman Historians

Other than the works of the panegyrists there survives no contemporary record of the events relating to Britain. The earliest surviving histories which make reference to the Carausian episode are those given by two later historians, Aurelius Victor and Eutropius.

Sextus Aurelius Victor was an African who was appointed Governor of *Pannonia Secunda* in 361, and *Praefectus Urbi* in 389. He published his history *Caesares* sometime after 360. Eutropius, who accompanied Julian on his Persian Campaign in 363, wrote his history sometime shortly after 364.

Both these writers are distanced by more than seventy years from the reign of Carausius, but it is likely that they would have had reasonable contemporary records on which to draw. Both writers agree on many points. Victor states that Carausius was a native of Menapia: the Menapians being a seafaring people who had settled the coastal area between the Rhine and the Scheldt. Webb (Webb 1907) puts forward the suggestion that there were many Menapian trading stations around the British coast, and even in Ireland and the Isle of Man. His source of information on this point is unquoted, but the lack of contemporary archaeological evidence from Ireland (Mytum 1981) and the Isle of Man, however, does nothing to support such a suggestion, though Jannsens (Jannsens 1937) expands the unconvincing argument for the Emperor's Manx descent. Victor adds that Carausius distinguished himself by his feats of valour, and that he was also skilled in nautical matters, having been a pilot in his youth. He also states that Carausius was overthrown by the guile of his first minister Allectus after six years.

Eutropius (Translation by Thomas 1760) gives his account in *Liber ix*, 22-23. He also gives some detail of the early career of Carausius. *"...Carausius, who though very ignobly descended, had acquired a great reputation in a considerable post in the army, having received a commission at Bononia to make all quiet at sea along the coasts of Belgica and Amorica, which the Franks and*

Saxons had infested. Frequently taking several of the Barbarians, but neither returning the booty to the provincials, nor sending it to the Emperors, a suspicion being entertained that he let the Barbarians designedly into the Empire, that in their return with plunder he might pick them up..... Being ordered to be put to death by Maximian, he took the purple and seized Britain."
The commission received by Carausius is mentioned, but at no point is he recorded as having been bestowed with the expected title of *Praefectus* (Starr 1960).

This story of Carausius keeping the plunder occurs very often in later works, though the apparent acceptance of the British population of his take-over makes it likely that they were oblivious to any of the dubious activities mentioned above. It is a distinct possibility that Maximian may have been wary or even jealous of any success gained by Carausius, this forming the origin of the above accusations.

Eutropius then places the British rebellion as contemporary with several other events upsetting the peace of the central empire. These include the revolt of Achilleus in Egypt, (296), the infestation of North Africa by the *Quinegentiani*, and the kindling of war in the east by the Sasanian leader Narseh (Sellwood 1985), (Plate 2 nos.11-12). He also concedes that Carausius was well skilled in military matters, and informs us of the 'peace' concluded with Maximian and Diocletian.
He concludes that *"Allectus, an associate of his, slew him seven years after, and kept possession of Britain after him for three years, but was at last quelled by the conduct of Asclepiodotus, prefect of the guards. Thus Britain was recovered in the tenth year after it was lost."*

This gives us some further ideas on the chronology of the revolt. Combining the versions of Eutropius, Victor and the information tendered by the second panegyric, a possible framework of events could be :-

Late 286......Carausius declares himself emperor at Rouen

Early 287.....Carausius moves to Britain. Rouen is lost shortly after.

Summer 289....Maximian's recovery force defeated by the elements, Carausian naval power or a combination of both.

290-291......A negotiated peace settlement agreed, with Carausius maintaining power in Britain.

Jan/Feb 293....Carausius overthrown by Allectus, who immediately tries to gain a continental foothold at Boulogne.

March/April 293....Boulogne besieged by Constantius, and is soon captured.

Summer 296.......Britain retaken by Asclepiodotus.

These figures tie in with the historians' accounts of events. The province is recovered in the tenth year after it was lost. Allectus keeps possession of *Britannia* for three years, and the reign of Carausius was ended in its seventh year.

The Scottish Chroniclers

One must avoid *" the attempt to shore up imprecise data by historical speculation masquerading as certainty"*

R.F.J.Jones. CHANGE ON THE FRONTIER: Northern Britain in the Third Century. King & Henig. B.A.R.109ii. 1981

Two mediaeval Scottish chroniclers have left full accounts of the life of Carausius, and although their accuracy on many points may be questionable, they do yield some information, not mentioned in the earlier sources, that may be worthy of consideration. The works undoubtedly contain much fiction and have a generally nationalistic flavour, but nevertheless contain enough accuracy in many of these areas discussed by the earlier historians to make a detailed reading and reasoned assessment worthwhile. Much Celtic folklore dates back many centuries, for example the *Dream of Macsen Wledig* from the Welsh *Mabinogion* (Jones and Jones 1993) alludes to the time of Magnus Maximus 383-8. Though such folklore is much distorted and elaborated, a few elements still remain in the works of the Scottish historians which deserve further attention.

John of Fordun is believed to have written *Chronica Gentis Scotorum* in the fourteenth century, although claims have been made that it is a much later work. James Watson, for example (Watson 1886), makes a fascinatingly eccentric attempt to discredit the work of Fordun as a Post-Reformation Forgery. None of these claims are strong enough to persuade one to ignore the content of Fordun completely, and the main points incorporated in his work are outlined below.

Fordun follows Eutropius closely and speaks of the *vilissime natus* of Carausius. He agrees that Carausius held Britain for seven years before being killed by Allectus who then held Britain for a further three years. The novel addition that Fordun makes to the story is mention of Carausius ceding land to the Scots in some sort of deal. This is also mentioned by the second Scottish chronicler, Hector Boethius.

The Bodlean Library in Oxford contains a facsimile of the work of Hector Boethius, *Chronicles of Scotland*, 1540, which was printed in Amsterdam in 1977. This facsimile differs in some places from *Boece's History of Scotland* in the Mar Lodge Translation, (Watson 1946), which relies heavily on a transcription carried out by John Bellenden in 1685.

With regard to the origins of Carausius, the Bellenden transcription states, " *Ffor Carance (quham Eutropius callis Cawras).......he was repute be Romanis of obscure origin (for he dis-symulit his kin).....".* It then refers to his early career as follows..." *in Illyric, Gallia and Italie he conquest grete renown."* The Amsterdam facsimile agrees on the career of Carausius, *".......wa gret honouris i Italie,"* but resorts at this point to nationalistic fiction giveing Carausius a Scottish origin, and even royal lineage, referring to *"Carance the second brother of Findok."* This version follow a path well-trodden in folklore speaking of Carausius leaving his homeland in disgrace and joining the Roman legions after being implicated in the death of his brother.

Both versions agree closely on the events leading up to the assumption of the purple, the quotes used here being taken from the Amsterdam facsimile. Both versions agree that Carausius was sent by Diocletian to defend the coasts of Normandy and Picardy (but not Britain) from pirates, and speak of his keeping the spoils without sending a share to the emperor, describing his ships thus..."*Thay was ladyn ful of riches and guddis.."* . Accused of treason Carausius flees to Britain, but his landing there is treated in a most unexpected way."*...(He) come with weirmen and riches and lands in Westmureland ane part of Britane nocht far fra the landis of Scottis and Pichtis..."*

The commentary continues with talk of the power of the Romans already in Britain being on the wane. It describes Carausius enlisting the help of both Scots and Picts, before marching towards York. It describes a great battle taking place not far from York. "*..In yis batall wer slane Quintus Bassianus Capitane of Britane, and Hirci(us) procurator with mony othir nobillis and commonis of thair blude.......and tuke ye sceptour and diademe of Britane contrar the Empire of Romanis, iiicxlvi yeris.."*

This gives a date for the battle and ensuing events. The date is made clearer in the Mar Lodge transcription......"*He tuke ye purpure and crowne of Britane, iijcxlvi yere eftir be Iulius Cesare was to Romanis made tributare."* Caesar was made military tribune in 72 B.C. so this event makes an unlikely starting point. His first consulship was in 60 B.C., however, and this could well be the starting point referred to. Three hundred and forty six years from this point would take the dating to 287, there being no year zero. This would fit in well with the theory of initial usurpation at Rouen in 286, followed by landings and complete control of Britain in 287. There may well be more than a grain of truth in this version, although it would very likely be the case that Carausius had already landed in the South of England and gained the support of legionaries based there before sailing to Westmoreland, and marching on York. A significant factor may be revealed in the coinage. Carausius commemorates many legions on his coinage, many of which were stationed far away from Britain, although detachments from any of these legions may have formed part of the Carausian forces, but one legion not cited on any coin is the VI *Victrix*, known to have been stationed at York. Caution must, however, be

exercised here. The VI *Victrix* Legion was probably transferred to Britain in 119 (Frere 1967) and stationed at York. Records for the military presence in Britain in the late third century are lacking, and though no absolutely firm proof exists that they were still present in York in 287, this must remain a distinct possibility. The naming of Quintus Bassianus and Hircius as Captain and Procurator is also of interest. Though Shiel (Shiel 1977) points out that the name may refer to a confused account of Caracalla's earlier campaigns in the North, c.210, there is no obvious reason to assume that such a name would be uncommon enough not to reappear in the annals of Roman Britain.

Boethius then gives details of the deal made with the Scots and Picts..." *The remanent Scottis and Pychtys returnit hame richit with the spulze of this last batall. Than Carance in more princely reward of thair laubouris gaif all the landis iyland betuix the wall of Adriane and Yorke namyt Westmureland and Cumber to thair perpetuall dominioun..."* The Carlisle milestone, however, proves that this was not wholly true. This sole piece of surviving epigraphic evidence of the reign gives us firm proof that the area up to the wall was still under the authority and control of Carausius, and remained so after the retaking of Britain by Constantius in 296. Archaeological evidence, discussed later, does, however, seem to indicate a running down of manpower assigned to the wall at about this time. This, together with new hostility towards Constantius on the part of the Northern tribes,may well have necessitated the rebuilding work on the wall commencing about 296 (Breeze 1982).

It is possible that the sense in which *dominioun* is used in the passage quoted above may refer to some sort of free-trade area or agreement, allowing Picts and Scots free access as far south as York. Such an agreement would certainly be in the interest of Carausius, since a relatively peaceful north of Britain would allow more deployment of troops to the south, from whence any invasion may be expected to come.

Several Carausian coins have appeared at the site of Traprain Law, (Schulla1982) and one also at Newstead in Roxburghshire(Smith 1854), the negligible intrinsic value of these *antoniniani* indicating that they probably arrived in the course of trade, rather than as plunder. The importance of Traprain Law as a trading centre is also well attested (Breeze *ibid*).

The works attributed to Boethius also give a slightly different slant on the motives of Allectus. The assassination of Carausius is described simply in the Amsterdam facsimile.. "*...he held the crowne of Britane by crafty prudance qui hil at last he wes slane the vii yeir of his regne by Alectus, Romane capitane.."* This version does not dwell upon Allectus's motives as does the Mar Lodge translation...." *(Carance) was slane be tresson of Alect, quihilk of subtile and wylye ingyne come in Britane.."* This gives an indication that Allectus came to

Britain, or was sent by Central Empire in order to cause insurrection. The Amsterdam facsimile seems to support the second possibility, suggesting that Allectus did not immediately take the purple, but tried to return the Britons to the authority of Rome. " *This Alectus eftir the slaucht of Carance set his extreme besynes to bryng the Britonis agane to Romane lawis.And quhe he saw thay mycht na wayis be brocht thairto, for the cruell hatrent thay had aganis Romanis, he made laubouris to have thair benivolence and finalie appladit to yair opinioun and tuk the crowne of Britane, contrar the auctorite of Romanis...*"

The end of the breakaway empire is then recorded thus..".."*...he was slane be Asclepiadotus in the iii yeir of his regne.........eftir quhais deith ye crowne of Britane was restorit (as it was afore) to the Romanis.*"

The works of the Scottish chroniclers need to be treated with caution, but enough of the information tendered is of sufficient accuracy to necessitate the otherwise unrecorded items to be treated seriously. Some of these may well have been passed down in folklore over hundreds of years before Fordun and Boethius compiled their works.

Chapter Three

Archaeological Evidence from Late Third Century Britain

Any discussion pertaining to the use of the coinage, should be made in conjunction with the archaeological evidence available. Archaeological evidence from the last decade of the third century is often dependent on coin finds so that the two are inextricably linked. Archaeological evidence from this decade is somewhat limited, but even so, that which is available can give us valuable information.

This survey will aim to collate evidence from around Britain and thus create a picture of possible activity in the province just prior to, and during, the British Empire. For convenience London is treated as a special case being the capital of the province, followed by separate sections on military and civil sites, though by the end of the third century it appears that the two had often mingled, as at Piercebridge where a 'fort' had been built alongside a thriving town (Jones 1981).

LONDON

That London, as capital of the province, was the most important and populous town in Britain is not open to question. It is almost certain that Carausius would have located his main administration here, and as a result the city would have in all probability housed the main treasury and a mint.

Archaeological evidence from third century London has been scant, but recent work in the South-west corner of the Roman city has yielded some interesting results (Williams 1993). The excavations brought to light some massive foundations. Williams comments, " *It is unlikely that the complex was purely military, being upstream of the bridge, and poorly positioned to defend London, but the monumental size and elaborate nature of its construction suggest that it was intended to form an impressive monument, dominating the waterfront."*

Several of the wooden piles used in the foundations were rescued and dated by dendrochronology. Such a method, not withstanding the possibility of systematic errors caused by external influences, can be extremely accurate, and in this case it was used to date the commencement of the structure to 294, making the project a *"last flourishing of the so called British Empire."*

Williams has postulated that, *"Allectus, whose base is thought to have been London may have been seeking to construct a palace, mint, treasury and supply base complex, along lines common with the reorganised late third century (central) empire."* It is at this stage worth considering if there is any numismatic evidence which may coincide with such a scheme.

Although there is no direct evidence of the complex

housing a mint, such a building scheme would undoubtedly cause a reorganisation of the administration, and a knock-on effect may well be mirrored in a reorganisation of the coinage. The introduction of the 'quinarius' by Allectus may thus be possibly construed as being linked to this activity in the capital.

Major building work is often represented on the coinage of the Roman Empire, and architectural types often match with present day archaeological evidence. The *ROMAE AETER(N)* types of Allectus, showing a temple (R.I.C. 40 and 113), readily spring to mind. It may be construed as significant that a similar type was issued under Carausius (R.I.C.389), and that this coin, on the basis of its index mark *S/P/C* is dated to the very end of his reign. The possibility must thus be considered that a temple dedicated to Roma could have been part of this, or some other contemporary building programme.

Since the latter two coins emanate from the C mint, this could provide evidence of both L and C coins being issued from the London mint, a possibility discussed in detail later.

A previously unrecorded reverse type, (Plate 3. No.14), showing a hexastyle temple is worthy of note. The reverse legend is *VRBIS AVG*, and inside the temple is the inscription *MVLTIS IMP*. The exergual mark reads *RES*. The obverse style is orthodox. The town of the emperor so mentioned is in all probability London, and the enigmatic *RES* may well be an abbreviation for *RESTITVTOR*. It is tempting to suppose that such a legend, *RestitutorUrbis Augusti*, refers to public works instigated by Carausius at London.

It is easy to become over enthusiastic about such ideas, and to attempt to read too much into a coinage type, and such thoughts should be tempered with caution on two counts. Firstly, R.I.C.578, a silver 'denarius' of Carausius, shows a similar type and legend, but bears the index mark *RSR*, and must thus be dated to early in the reign. Secondly the type is almost identical to the reverse used by earlier emperors notably Probus on their coinages, and as a result may be little more than a copy of this earlier type.

The importance of London as an administrative centre is supported by this archaeological evidence, and an impressive rebuilding scheme, which may never have come to full fruition, initiated by Carausius and continued by Allectus seems a likely possibility.

MILITARY SITES

A discussion of military activity, or lack of it, during the

British Empire requires examination of evidence from three quite different areas. Firstly, it requires an appraisal of the activity on the northernmost boundary of the empire, a consideration of the deployment of troops to the area of Hadrian's Wall and the northern hinterland, including military sites along the two northern coasts. Secondly, there exists the problematical nature, dating and use of the southern coastal defences or Saxon Shoreline as it is sometimes, perhaps misleadingly, called. Finally, there remains the issue of military deployment in Wales during the late third century. Archaeological evidence from these areas may be used to build up a possible picture of activity during the reign of Carausius.

The second half of the third century was, for the Roman Empire in general, a time of much discord and strife. There were many frontier wars to be fought, but the greatest danger came from within the empire itself. During these troubled years a succession of generals and military leaders made attempts at securing the purple by military means. This led to fighting which weakened the military strength of the empire as revolts and breakaway 'empires' flourished. Britain was one of the few parts of the empire to remain fairly unaffected by these upheavals.

The Wall was very far removed from these troubles and *"the civil wars passed by and the frontier remained peaceful,"* (Breeze and Dobson 1987). There are no contemporary reports of hostile activity from over the border at this time, and it is likely that the manpower required to garrison the Wall had been substantially run down. Although this has often been interpreted as an excuse for the Picts to attack the Wall installations, and there is evidence of fire at several sites, there is no evidence that this was caused by attack rather than by innocent means. The panegyrics do not suggest any hostility with the Picts before the second visit of Constantius in 306, and the Scottish historians even suggest a pact with Carausius. It is likely that some of the forts fell quickly into disrepair. Excavations at Halton Chesters (Gillam 1961) and at Rudchester (Gillam 1972) both indicate that many buildings inside these forts lay in ruins by the end of the third century, even though there is strong evidence of a continued if skeletal occupation throughout the period. This is provided by the *Notitia Dignitatum* which indicates old style units still in residence during the fourth century. An inscription from Birdoswald commemorating rebuilding work, probably shortly after 296 indicates similar problems.

PRAETORVM QVOD ERAT HVMO COPERTVM ET IN LABEM CONLAPSVM ET PRINCIPIA ET BALNEVM RESTIVIT.

He restored the commanding officer's house which had been covered with earth and fallen into ruin, and the Headquarters building and a bath building.

At Bewcastle, the excavation report states, with some concern, that not a single coin of Carausius or Allectus was present in the level of occupation. The report failed to consider the possibility that the occupation may well have ceased before 286 (Gillam 1974).

The units in the Wall forts may well have shrunk to very low numbers, in those forts maintaining occupation, by the end of the third century, and it is possible that unscrupulous officers were making some profit out of drawing dead mens' pay (Breeze and Dobson *ibid*). That there was a run-down of troop strength rather than complete withdrawal may be inferred from the *Notitia Dignitatum,* which lists seven old style units, which presumably remained, even if in token strength, during this period, and also fourteen new style units housed in forts presumably abandoned in the latter half of the third century. There is every likelihood that these troop withdrawals coincide with peace on the frontier although the civilian settlement at Vindolanda may well, on the basis of coin evidence, also have been abandoned about the same time.

Daniels has suggested that the run-down may have been due to the removal of troops to fight in foreign wars or to build the city walls in southern Britain, many of which appear to date from around 270, or even to help in the construction of the Saxon Shore (Daniels 1980).

It has sometimes been suggested that Allectus stripped the wall of much of its remaining strength in preparation for his final battle, but modern evidence seems to indicate that the wall was manned at a very low level, even before Carausius's reign began.

As illustrated by Vindolanda, civil settlements often grew alongside the forts. At Carlisle the settlement, which together with the fort seems to have kept a moderate level of occupation throughout the period, grew to encompass seventy acres. At Corbridge, where a town of thirty acres grew around the site of possibly a legionary base depot, the Carausian coin evidence is fairly strong, with 169 coins of the British Empire representing 3.9 % of the total. Put into context by comparing the British Empire coins at the site with those of the Gallic Empire, although Corbridge seems to have remained busy, activity does seem to have declined slightly during the intervening years (Bishop and Dore 1988).

There is also evidence of a run-down of manpower on the North-West coast about this time. Coin evidence from Ravenglass for Carausian times is non-existent and the fort may have ceased to be occupied by this stage. There is again some evidence of fire at Ravenglass about this time (Cherry 1979), but Cherry concludes that " *it could have been caused by enemy attack or sea-borne enemies..., it may also have been a purely accidental fire unrelated to the times."* As regards the possibility of sea-borne attackers from Ireland troubling the coast at this time; "*if the Irish people had been heavily involved with raiding in the late third century, we should expect to find more evidence of it in Ireland itself,"* (Mytum 1981). It may, of course, be argued that the debased bronze coinage available in Britain at this time would be of little intrinsic worth to such raiders when compared to more valuable but perishable commodities as slaves. A case for Irish raiders was put forward by Simpson (Simpson 1964), in an effort to explain Carausian hoards from Wales which are usually from coastal areas. This must meet with the same arguments as applied to Ravenglass. It must remain conjectural whether the Irish had yet developed the maritime technology and navigational prowess to cross the Irish Sea with the accuracy required in a raid. Furthermore it seems unlikely that debased and intrinsically worthless coins should be hidden from the Irish raiders rather than silver and gold jewellery and tableware. Even in the fourth century when gold and silver was more readily available to raiders there is little to be found in Ireland, save the deposits at Newgrange which in all probability are votive in nature. It is also relevant that whereas the Isle of Man is an ideal stopping-off point for raiders plundering the North-West coast, there is hardly any Roman material found there. The need for defence on this coast in the late third century was in all probability an unnecessary luxury that was gradually removed.

Piercebridge in the hinterland of the Wall shows evidence of a thriving civilian settlement dating from perhaps the late first century. The fort at Piercebridge was for many years considered to be dated to the campaigns of Constantius I (Frere 1974). More recent evidence shows, however, that the fort, although the term 'fort' may be somewhat loosely used in this context, is more likely to have its origins about 270, and no evidence of an earlier fort has appeared (Jones 1981). The possibility of the fort actually being some form of fortified supply depot or warehouse serving the wall must be considered. The 138 Carausian coins from Piercebridge (Casey and Brickstock to be published), indicate its activity at the time. In a similar way the fort at Newton Kyme, a few miles west of York, has for many years also been considered to be the work of Constantius I, but the dating and significance of the site is far from clearly understood at present.

Activity in the south of Britain at this time is at present under re-evaluation. Both J. C. Mann and S. Johnson judge that the construction of the forts at Richborough and Lympne began before the time of Carausius (Maxfield 1989). This is supported by the coin evidence. They suggest that others such as Porchester may have been added in Carausian times, and that only Pevensey seems to be of a later date. Though, in the light of recent excavations at Pevensey, a Carausian dating may also be possible here (Fulford in discussion 1995). Brancaster and Reculver are enigmatic, on style alone they may be thought of as earlier, but Mann warns that building style alone is no guarantee of dating, and suggests that they may well fit in as contemporary with the others.

Richborough is by far the most productive site in Britain

for Carausian coins, though in context the 1173 coins of Carausius and 260 of Allectus, only form just over 3% of the over 50,000 identified coins from the site (Reece 1981). What is much more revealing, however, is the fact that the ratio of British Empire: Gallic Empire coins is at 0.55 the highest of any major site in the country, excluding Portchester which is itself an exceptional case. This must illustrate the importance of Richborough to Carausius and mirror the intense activity taking place there during the British Empire. It is likely that at, or about, this time a large part of the 2nd Augustan Legion was relocated from Caerleon to Richborough. This is discussed in greater detail later in this chapter.

The fort at Portchester may well have been commenced in Carausian times, (Cunliffe 1975). The coins of Carausius are abundant and are often in unworn condition. There are also radiates present, but many are in worn condition and these may well have spent the intervening years in circulation. The ratio of coins of Carausius to those of Allectus at 54:2 is extraordinarily high (Reece in Cunliffe *ibid)*. The numismatic indication is that Portchester was indeed probably commenced at about the start of the reign of Carausius, although the apparent lack of activity under Allectus is somewhat mystifying.

For many years, the purpose of the Saxon Shore forts has been seen as that of military and naval police-stations used to deter or repel Saxon pirates. This view has been questioned by Johnson (Johnson in Maxfield1989). Cotterill has put forward some arguments against the main use of the forts being that of the control of Saxon pirates (Cotterill 1993). Cotterill points out that the logistics of crossing to Britain in an open rowing boat would have involved a long and somewhat haphazard journey of limited navigational accuracy, unless the crossing were made across the Straits of Dover. Even at this point, such a return journey would take upwards of sixteen hours, under favourable conditions.

It is worthy of note that there are no contemporary references to raiding on Britain, though the Roman historians make it clear that one of the tasks of Carausius was to rid the coasts of Northern Gaul of such pirates. Raiding of Northern Gaul, including incursions upstream of the main navigable rivers would undoubtedly constituted easier missions for the pirates to undertake.

The actual spacing of the forts would again make observation and cutting off of such intruders no means certain. Evidence of Saxon raiding at this time has been based on large Gallic Empire hoards being buried in the South-East of Britain (Frere 1967), but this is more likely to reflect the population concentration in Britain, and the relative worthlessness of the currency leading to non-recovery (Robertson 1988). The idea has been put forward that the forts were actually trans-shipment centres and as such were worthy of protection by a military garrison. They would, as such, be used for the collection, storage and shipment of state supplies (Milne 1990).

This argument does, however, fail to justify their obvious activity during the Carausian regime when the import and export of goods to and from the continent was likely to be minimal, excepting of course any foothold that Carausius may have held on the continent. An argument could, indeed, be put forward that if this were the use of the forts, then a foothold on the continent must have been held for a sizeable portion of the reign of Carausius. There is also a more plausible explanation of their use at this time. Carausius would have known that Central Empire would almost certainly plan an invasion and retaking of Britain. Such an invasion would be likely to take place along the coast in question, and whatever the prior and later use of the stations might have been, it is likely that Carausius would have deployed defensive troops and ships at these sites. The panegyric states that Carausius *"carried off the fleet that defended the Gauls and then built a host of ships himself."* These would have been located around the south and east coasts to with the priority of repelling any invasion from Gaul.

The importance of naval power to Carausius is well-reflected on the coinage. Galleys appear on coins of the *C* mint (R.I.C.264-5), the *RSR* mint (R.I.C.560 and 606-7), at Rouen (R.I.C. 635-6 and 648-9) and also on the unmarked coinage (R.I.C.779). It is of interest to note that no Galley coins of Carausius appear at the *L* mint, although this omission is certainly well rectified under Allectus. Naval power is also represented on the enigmatic *PACATRIX AVG CANC* coin, showing a fine ship, now in the Ashmolean Museum (Sutherland 1937).

The military sites in Wales, and close to its borders, at the end of the third century require special consideration. Caerleon, the legionary fortress of the Second Augustan Legion shows evidence of having been run down about this time. Boon suggests that about this time a decided change took place in the occupation of the fortress. The levelling and dismantlement of buildings suggest that it was no longer required. Recent excavations have done much to support the traditional view that the legion was removed at some moment of crisis in perhaps 293, never thereafter to return in strength (Boon in Jarrett 1969). In some ways this seems to mirror the withdrawal of troops from the Wall, and it appears that the bulk of the legion may have been transferred to Richborough about this time, with the possibility that many of the troops were used in an abortive foray to the continent in 293.

At Chester, the other legionary fortress on the borders of Wales there are again signs of dismantling of buildings. There are, however, some important differences. At Caerleon, both the *principia* and the *praetorium* were dismantled, but at Chester this was not the case, and these buildings continued to be occupied (Strickland 1981). Strickland puts forward the possibility that the fortress may have become a fleet base about this time. If this were

the case, then it would mirror the conjectured use of the Saxon Shore forts at the time. The last official mention of the Legion XX *Valeria Victrix* in Britain occurs on an inscription (RIB1956), dated to about 260. Lack of written evidence should not make us discount the likelihood that at least some part of the legion remained in Chester after this date. The fact that Carausius issued coins in the name of that legion, showing its badge of a boar, can be construed to indicate their continued presence in Britain in at least some form at this time (Plate 7 No.1). The coin evidence from Chester certainly echoes the idea of a continued occupation into Carausian times (personal inspection at Chester Museum). Although the level of occupation would, in parallel with Caerleon, have been reduced to little more than a token garrison under Allectus.

Other military sites in Wales do not, however, fit well into this picture of withdrawal and run-down. Coin evidence from the excavations at *Segontium* shows a continuity of occupation from about 80 to beyond the reign of Magnus Maximus (Casey *et al* 1993). The key to this fact may well be that as well as having an excellent position, overlooking the Menai Straits and the island of Anglesey with its fertile land and also its important copper deposits, the fort could receive shipments of supplies easily by sea.

Mark Curteis (*ibid*) has calculated that the garrison in Carausian times may have been about 150, and that numerically there was little change from the Gallic Empire. The method employed uses a knowledge of Army pay and an estimate of likely garrison strength at an earlier stage, together with coin loss to calculate the strength.

One has to treat any such calculation with reserve, and there are, as with most statistical methods, some inherent shortcomings present. The assumption that rate of coin loss would be constant is itself open to question since an inflated brass two-denarius piece of the Gallic Empire would be unlikely to justify the same effort of recovery, if lost, as a silver denarius would have done some century earlier. It is also possible since Gallic coins formed part of the currency pool in Carausian times, that the picture may be distorted, and that there was actually an increase in activity that followed a partial run-down in the 270's. Nevertheless, such a method is a good starting point for such calculations, and it reinforces the likelihood that the garrison strength at *Segontium* was not run down in keeping with the two legionary fortresses. The concept of the fort being part of a maritime supply network should also be considered.

Lydney has produced many coins of the British Empire, a fact discussed later in connection with the unusually high numbers of coins from the *C* mint present. It is not inconceivable that the Roman fleet may have had a base, as yet undetected, in the area. A connection between the Roman Fleet, and the Bristol Channel is suggested by a

FIGURE 2 POSSIBLE WEST COAST MARITIME SUPPLY ROUTE

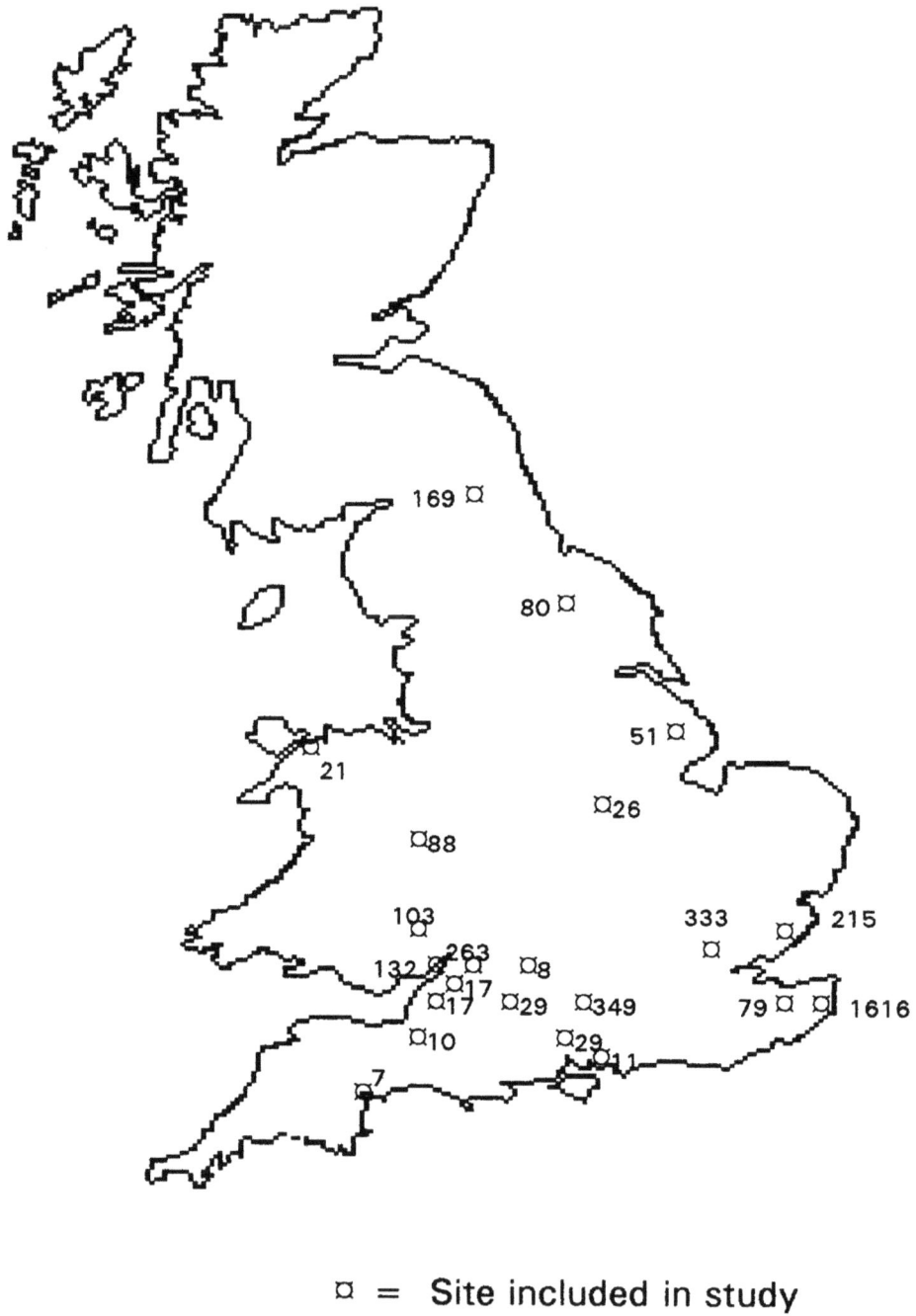

FIGURE 3 MAP OF MAJOR SITE FINDS OF CARAUSIUS AND ALLECTUS
The number shown refers to the number of British Empire coins found on that site.

pavement from the great temple complex at Lydney, dedicated by a man whose official title was shortened to *PR.REL.*, which has been interpreted as *Praefectus Reliquationis Classis,* or the person in charge of a fleet supply base, with the likelihood that the base lay nearby, (Johnson 1980).

The new style fort at Cardiff closely resembles the plan of that at Portchester, and may well have been operational about the same time.

Further west, excavations on the sites of earlier forts at Neath and Loughor, both on navigable estuaries, have both produced evidence of late third century reoccupation, (Davies 1991). Though coin evidence at Neath is scant, there is little doubt of some activity in the area in Carausian times, as the Neath Hoard testifies (Taylor 1930).

The discovery of a Romano-Celtic boat at Magor, Gwent (Nayling *et al.* 1994), which may have been deliberately sunk for use as a jetty, again gives evidence of nautical activity along the South Welsh coast during the period in question, an antoninianus of Carausius being recovered from alongside the vessel, albeit unstratified.

Thus there must exist the possibility of a network of maritime installations around the Welsh coastline with any or all of these sites *viz.* Gloucester/Lydney, Cardiff, Neath, Loughor, Caernarfon and Chester, playing a part. Carmarthen, on the mouth of the Towy, could also have formed part of such a scheme. Pennal, is also well situated on the tidal reaches of the Dyfi, and any evidence of late third century activity here could strongly reinforce the concept of such a maritime supply route requiring a chain of shore installations. Descriptions by earlier writers suggest that the site at Pennal was important enough to have been walled, and suggest a possible site for both a bath building and a *vicus* (Bowen and Gresham 1967 and Irvine 1958). Such a chain could then progress along the north-west coast up to the Solway Firth to serve Carlisle and the remnants of the Wall garrison (fig.2). As stated previously it is unlikely that the danger from Irish raiders was acute enough to demand a network of forts around the relatively sparsely populated Welsh coastline, and defence would not seem to be the prime use of such installations.

The other major anomaly in military deployment in Wales seems to have been the reoccupation of several inland forts. At Caerhun, *"the (coin) list reaches its greatest density in the late third century, a phenomenon to be associated with the usurpation of Carausius,"* (Casey in Jarrett, ibid.). A similar pattern may be discerned in the numismatic evidence from Brecon Gaer and Castell Collen, while at Caersws, late third century pottery illustrates a continuance of occupation. A mystery still remains as to why such forts were reoccupied at this stage, though Davies suggests that the garrisoning of both Caersws and Brecon Gaer might have been linked with

that at Caernarfon (Davies ibid.). The idea of trouble from local tribes in such a sparsely populated area is unlikely at such a late stage in the Romanisation of Britain, while the simple necessity of housing the troops of Carausius, including those brought from the continent is too simplistic a solution. A more logistically sound reason may well be that Caerhun is well placed on the overland supply route to Caernarfon, that Caersws is on the direct route from Wroxeter to Pennal, and that Brecon Gaer is equally well placed on the route to Carmarthen or the gold mines at Dolaucothi.

CIVIL SETTLEMENTS

Some of the northern settlements are, as has been mentioned earlier, inextricably intertwined with military installations. If the Wall garrisons were run down at some time after 270, then it should then follow that the adjacent civilian townships should suffer a linked drop in prosperity. There would also be a strong likelihood of a drifting southward of the general population towards established settlements where the people would be more likely to make a living income. One would thus expect to find an increase in population in the hinterland towns such as Piercebridge, Catterick and Aldborough. This does appear to be the case, and is discussed more fully later in this chapter.

Since virtually all towns in Roman Britain show continuous occupation throughout the second half of the third century and the first half of the fourth century, then coin finds from the respective sites may furnish us with much useful information about their relative prosperity in Carausian times. Any statistical method is likely to be clouded by systematic faults, but even so may yield some support for direct archaeological evidence. By comparing the coin yield from two virtually adjacent periods it should be possible to gain a perception of the relative activities of a group of towns. The choice of adjacent periods should minimise the effect of any major social change occurring at the site. The argument put forward that coin loss depends on squalor of habitation, (i.e. more rubbish produced yields more coin loss (Reece 1991)), should again, for these adjacent periods be minimised, if indeed any effect is likely to be present over so short a time span. The following table (fig.4) compares the finds of Gallic Empire coins from twenty three sites, with finds of British Empire coins. The Gallic Empire totals consist, as best as can be differentiated from coin lists in some instances, of official coins. The production of the unofficial radiate coinage took place over a substantial time and regional variations in numbers make its exclusion a safer option. Though the official radiates remained in circulation throughout the British Empire, as the Blackmoor hoard almost certainly indicates, the effect on a simple ratio test should not in any way cloud the results. All the sites chosen have yielded over four hundred and fifty recorded coins, and are thus likely to have yielded fairly representative samples. In any analysis of the results, caution must be exercised in dealing with sites producing low numbers of coins in any

SITE	British	Gallic	Total	%BE	BE:GE
PORCHESTER	56	23	603	9.3	2.43
RICHBOROUGH	1616	2939	51726	3.1	0.55
ALDBOROUGH	80	151	1283	6.2	0.53
CIRENCESTER	263	513	6606	4.0	0.51
SILCHESTER	349	721	6367	5.5	0.48
SEGONTIUM	21	46	1071	2.0	0.46
LAMYATT BEACON	29	63	1378	2.1	0.46
LINCOLN	51	137	1264	4.0	0.37
WANBOROUGH	38	119	1753	2.2	0.32
LEICESTER	26	89	706	3.7	0.29
LYDNEY	132	461	6209	2.1	0.29
VERULAMIUM	333	1171	6100	5.4	0.28
WROXETER	88	325	2636	3.3	0.27
WINCHESTER	29	120	792	3.6	0.24
COLCHESTER	215	903	5435	4.0	0.24
CANTERBURY	79	326	1845	4.3	0.24
ILCHESTER	10	49	370	2.7	0.20
CORBRIDGE	169	850	4285	3.9	0.19
LOWBURY HILL	8	49	877	0.9	0.16
CAMERTON	17	106	592	2.9	0.16
WEST PARK	11	73	724	1.5	0.15
EXETER	7	51	451	1.6	0.13
EASTON GREY	17	127	991	1.7	0.13
KENCHESTER	-	-	-	10.6	-

FIGURE 4 TABLE OF RATIOS OF BRITISH EMPIRE:GALLIC EMPIRE FINDS

category. For example any site yielding a mere 10 British Empire coins would have its figure changed by 10% by one undetected or even misattributed coin. Nevertheless, as stated before, the analysis can be a worthwhile exercise even for sites yielding low numbers of coin, and a far more reliable one for sites producing larger numbers of British Empire coins. The list of sites is placed in rank order for the ratio of British Empire coins: Gallic Empire coins. For comparison with the civil settlements the list also contains some military sites such as Portchester and Richborough, and also a selection of religious/temple sites such as Lydney and Lamyatt Beacon (Besly 1986). A list of the major settlements is summarised below.

SITE	STATUS	B:G RATIO
Aldborough	Tribal Capital	0.53
Cirencester	Tribal Capital	0.51
Silchester	Tribal Capital	0.48
Lincoln	Colonia	0.37
Wanborough	Major Settlement	0.32
Leicester	Tribal Capital	0.29
Verulamium	Tribal Capital	0.28
Wroxeter	Tribal Capital	0.27
Winchester	Tribal Capital	0.24
Colchester	Colonia	0.24
Canterbury	Tribal City	0.24
Ilchester	Town	0.20
Corbridge	Settlement	0.19
Camerton	Settlement	0.16
Exeter	Tribal Capital	0.13

The low ratio at Corbridge is in all likelihood a direct result of the run-down of the Wall garrisons discussed earlier. The number of coins found at Corbridge of Carausius and Allectus is substantial, 169 coins (Casey 1988), but when related to the large numbers of Gallic Empire coins the ratio is low for a town site, especially considering the continued military presence at the fort. Binchester seems to have suffered badly from this depopulation, a fact echoed in the rarity of British Empire coins from the site. Of 792 coins recorded from the site only two are issues of Carausius and none are of Allectus (Brickstock 1987).

The sites further south are much more productive. Both Piercebridge, discussed earlier, and Catterick (Casey forthcoming), yield substantial quantities of Carausian coin, whilst at Aldborough, the 80 British Empire coins represent a ratio of 0.53, the highest of any major civil site, and 6.2% of the total finds. The Aldborough coins, now in the care of English Heritage, represent a collection of finds on the site over many years, having been assembled by the landowners. As such, some caution must be exercised in ascertaining their relevance, since it is far likelier that common Gallic coins would be either given away as gifts or alternatively ignored. This may be a factor in creating such a high ratio of British:Gallic coins, but it is unlikely to play a major role.

On the basis of the coin evidence it seems probable that the run-down of military activity on the Wall caused a movement of civilian population southward with numbers settling into the townships along the major route away from the Wall. The apparent willingness of civilians to remain in towns not excessively far from the Wall does seem to indicate that there was little worry of Pictish incursions, and that the migration was primarily of economic necessity.

Lincoln, a *Colonia*, produces a high ratio of British:Gallic coins, (0.37). This may be indicative of increased economic activity in the area, though care must be taken in that the coin list includes coins from Lincoln in the City museum, which may be a selected rather than a true representation of all finds (Mann and Reece 1983).

A detailed survey of some 15,000 recorded Roman coin finds from Norfolk, (Davies and Gregory 1991), shows that two major sites, the Tribal Capital at Caistor-by-Norwich, and the settlement at Brampton, were active and thriving during the Carausian period.

Several large towns in the South-Eastern quarter of the province show remarkably similar patterns. The *Colonia* at Colchester, and the Tribal Capitals at *Verulamium*, Wroxeter, Winchester and Canterbury all show a ratio of between 0.24 and 0.28, and a percentage of total finds of British Empire coins of between 3.3% and 5.4%. The Tribal Capital at Leicester, with a ratio of 0.29, also seems to fit in with this pattern.

It is inherently dangerous to talk of an 'average' site, but this group of towns does seem to behave in such a way as to indicate that the Carausian usurpation affected them in a similar way.

The two Tribal Capitals most worthy of comment are Silchester and Cirencester. In each case the ratio of British:Gallic coins is extremely high. At Silchester it reaches 0.48, and at Cirencester 0.51. These two towns appear to behave in similar fashion, but in a significantly different way from other towns in Britain. It is of great significance that both lie on the main route West from London towards Wales. The probability therefore must exist that this increase in prosperity is directly linked to the increased military activity in Wales at the time. A counter argument that Silchester is also on a main route towards Bitterne on the South Coast, and that this is the major cause for increase in activity, may be negated by the fact that Winchester, also along this route, seems to behave in a totally orthodox way.

There is little direct evidence of archaeological form that can be dated accurately to this period. There is a likelihood that the last battle of the British Empire leading to the defeat of Allectus by Asclepiodotus, took place somewhere in this area, and according to Boon, *"Repairs to the South Tower may make the conception of a last stand not too wide of the mark,"* (Boon 1974). It is likely that the population of Silchester was somewhere in the region of 3000 to 8000 people, based on Boon's estimate *(ibid)* of about 4000.

The south-west of Britain, modern Devon and Cornwall, is virtually devoid of Roman activity, and the Tribal Capital at Exeter, the most westerly settlement of any size shows by far the lowest ratio at 0.13 of any of the major towns considered. This indicates that its relative importance, which had been on the wane for some time, had reached a low level.

Kenchester, near Hereford, on the Welsh border produces the most startling evidence of increased activity (Jack 1916 and 1926). Some 10.6% of the coin finds are of Carausius, a remarkably high total, though direct comparison with other sites must be avoided, since the percentage is dependent not only upon the nature of the site, but also on length of occupation of the site at any given level of population.

Alan Morris has put forward two possible reasons for this activity (Morris 1982). The first possibility being that in the troubled times of the late third century, the local population may have moved from the countryside into the relative safety of the town, or alternatively that the withdrawal of troops from Wales caused traders and camp followers to migrate eastwards behind the troops in order to carry on making a viable living. Both suggestions can be easily dismissed. There is, as mentioned earlier, little evidence of trouble from pirates or otherwise, and Kenchester, some thirty miles from the coast, would be unlikely to suffer such turmoil even if the possibility of sea-borne raiding existed. Secondly,

although the two legionary forts at Caerleon and Chester may have already been in the initial stages of a run-down, there is much evidence, outlined above, of increased military activity in Wales at this time. It seems much more likely, therefore, that the military activity that sparked this economic harvest for Kenchester was caused by the deployment of men and resources westward, rather than a withdrawal eastward. The fact that coinage was obviously flowing with some ease into Kenchester makes the likelihood of the boom being caused by a withdrawal less than likely.

The smaller agricultural sites in Wales also appear to be active at this stage. Cwm Brwyn in Dyfed has yielded a coin of Carausius (Ward 1906), and the hill-fort at Dinorben has produced seventeen Carausian coins, though interestingly none of Allectus (Gardner *et al.* 1964 and Savory 1971).

This relative paucity of Allectan coins in Wales is common to many sites, and may shed some evidence for withdrawals from Wales taking place under Allectus, in contrast to deployment of troops to the area under Carausius.

The general picture created of the province under Carausian rule seems to be a peaceful one, and despite the inflation rampant in the central Empire, one reflecting a certain amount of economic stability. It also seems likely that Carausius quickly created a shrewd, home-based administration system, using the manpower available to create efficient communication and good supply networks.

Chapter Four

The Production and Metrology of the Coinage

THE RADIATE COINAGE OF CARAUSIUS

The rapid production of coinage was a priority for any third-century usurper on his assumption of power. The necessity for a large, and almost immediate coinage was two-fold. In addition to the obligatory payment to the troops under his command, the coinage also provided an efficient and easily controlled propaganda medium, which could rapidly reach both the military and civil populations.

The monetary requirement of the military forces which supported the Carausian regime would have been considerable. Those troops that had given support to the rebellion would have expected pecuniary reward, as would any of the legionaries already based in Britain who had switched allegiance to the Carausian cause. The civilian population of Britain had been relatively fortunate during the second half of the third century, living in a peaceful outpost of the Empire that had, in all likelihood, escaped most of the violence generated by the power struggles of a succession of usurping generals. The raids of Saxon pirates formed the only possible cloud on an insular horizon, although some doubts have recently been cast as to whether any pirate raids actually took place on Britain at this time, or whether such attacks were merely confined to the other side of the English Channel (Cotterill 1993).

The urgent demand for coinage, would, in the short term, have been a problem for the new Emperor. Carausius had inherited a part of the Empire that did not already possess a mint, and the corresponding lack of mint administrators and production personnel would have needed to be rectified very quickly.

The demand for competent die-engravers would have had to be dealt with. It is unlikely that any engravers with experience of official mint production would have been available, and it is likely that the task may have been given, at least in part, to provincial gem-engravers who would have quickly needed to modify their techniques to coinage production (King 1985). Carausius may also have employed craftsmen with experience of the die-production for the barbarous radiate issues, some of whom were quite possibly still active in Britain, and a minority of whom had attained a degree of technical and artistic competence. Certainly some of the better executed reverse types on the radiates bear a similarity of style to that on certain Carausian issues, though not to an extent that provides more than tenuous support for this theory.

In order to ascertain the chronology of any coinage many factors have to be taken into account. Trends in style and metrology are key factors in the study of any coinage.

Alas, a study of die-linkage, which can provide the firmest of evidence, is a virtually impossible task on this particular coinage with its employment of literally thousands of dies. Much useful evidence can be gleaned through the study of hoard material, especially where the deposition date occurs within the reign itself. Two recently discovered hoards, discussed later, from Normanby (Bland and Burnett 1989) and Dorchester (King to be published), each contain thousands of coins terminating with a small number of Carausian pieces. It is thus highly likely that both hoards were buried very early in the reign, and as such they yield important information as to the constitution of the early coinage of Carausius.

The basis for the chronology of the coinage has been established over the years by Webb (Webb 1933) and Carson (Carson 1959 and 1971), but the recent hoard evidence and stylistic considerations both complement one another allowing reconsideration of these earlier works.

The *RSR* mark is now attested as appearing in hoards whose deposition date is likely to be near the start of the reign, as are several coins attributed to the 'Rouen' mint. This brings the dating of these two issues in the above works into question, and evidence now demands reconsideration of the whole chronology of the coinage.

Several coins exhibiting the *BRI* index mark have come to light in recent years. Their provenances are, however, well-spread (Wroxeter, Corbridge, Richborough (2), Strood, Chichester and Minchen Hole on the Gower Penninsula) giving no indication of the geographical location of the issuing mint (Shiel 1976, Shiel1979, and Boon 1994).

An estimated thirty to forty percent of Carausian bronze coins bear no index mark at all, and are referred to henceforth, as the unmarked types. Such coins are extremely common in early Carausian hoards, though unmarked coins of much finer style are often found in later hoards.

The fitting of the unmarked issues into the chronology poses a number of problems. It is likely, considering the number of surviving specimens, that the issue was prolonged over a large part of the reign. The style of the coins varies from the crude issues that seem to coincide with the beginning of the reign, through issues of style commensurate with that of the early issues of the *L* and *C* mints, and eventually concludes with large-flan, good-style issues typical of the later-middle period of the reign.

The grey area between official issues and unofficial and

barbarous imitations poses a particularly difficult problem in the study of the unmarked series. This problem is at its most acute during the first few months of the Carausian regime when the rapid need for coinage was a priority.

The actual location of the minting sites used by the Carausian administration has for many years been the subject of much discussion. It has been generally accepted that those coins bearing a mark of *L*, often in combination with other letters, were issued from a central mint based in *Londinivm*, but those bearing the mark *C*, again often in combination, have been attributed to *Cataractonivm* (Stukeley 1757), *Camvlodvnvm* (Webb 1933 and Askew 1951), or *Clavsentum* (Mattingly 1945) with *Glevvm* also being put forward as a tentative possibility on epigraphic grounds (Burnett and Casey1984).

The unmarked coinage has been attributed to a mint at Boulogne (Carson 1971), though this attribution was based on a very limited study of site-finds, which is not reinforced when a study is made of the distribution of these coins over the whole province. The whole question of the location of the minting centres now needs reappraisal.

Coins overstruck on those of earlier emperors form an interesting group, and the practice of overstriking previous issues seems quite common during the early part of the reign. Examples exist of not only the unmarked types, but also issues bearing the *L*, *C* and *RSR* marks. Enough examples of good style exist to indicate that official mint policy allowed use to be made of the flans of coins already in circulation. The under-types are often clearly visible and are usually of the later Gallic Emperors, Victorinus and the *Tetrici* Plate 7 No.16), or of Gallienus or Claudius *Gothicus*. Coins from as early as the reign of Philip I, 244-9, have, however, been found to have been restruck under Carausius. It is significant to note that overstriking seems most widespread during the early years of the reign but virtually dies out by its end. Overstrikes under Allectus are very rare, though there is an example in York Museum of an *antoninianus* of that emperor overstruck on one of Carausius (Plate 3 Nos.12-13).

Overstriking can produce some spectacular results. A fine example appeared in the Blackmoor Hoard, No.20439, showing the bust of Victorinus, apparently jugate with, and to the fore of that of Carausius. A similar coin from Lydney Park shows an apparently jugate bust of Tetricus I with that of Carausius (Plate 5 No.21). It is argued that the former cannot be a simple overstrike (Shiel 1975), since the bust of Victorinus was to the fore. This argument can be conclusively refuted by the coin illustrated (Plate 5 No.22) which shows a *DIVO CLAVDIO* posthumous issue of Claudius II, 268-70, overstruck on a lifetime issue of the same emperor. The earlier bust appears jugate and to the fore, thus verifying

the case of the two Carausian specimens being simple overstrikes.

Overstruck specimens, notably of the unmarked issues, present a further interesting problem. Some of these early types are quite barbarous in execution, but the very act of overstriking may be a significant factor in the argument for regarding such pieces as official. We have little idea of the official tariff of the early Carausian radiates, though their mix with Gallic Empire radiates in both early hoards, such as Normanby Bland and Burnett 1988) and Dorchester (King forthcoming), and in later hoards such as Blackmoor (Bland 1982) do indicate that they were probably tariffed at the same rate. Thus the profit margin for any forger using new dies to restrike old flans would be zero, and involve the unnecessary expenditure of both time and trouble in making the required dies. It would seem akin to a modern forger manufacturing new dies for one-pound coins and using them to strike blanks obtained from genuine one-pound coins taken out of circulation. This provides a logical reason for regarding overstruck coins as official issues. It may be argued that the Carausian pieces may have been tariffed at a higher rate than the Gallic radiates, perhaps in line with the Aurelianic standard used by the Central Empire. However, the supply of Aurelianic style coinage to Britain in the late 270's and early 280's seems on both hoard and site evidence to have been minimal, and the mixing of Carausian and Gallic Empire coinage in large hoards is well attested.

The fact that little overstriking seems to have taken place in the latter part of the reign when larger-flanned and better-struck coins were being produced could indicate the possibility that an attempt was made at this time to introduce a new standard in line with that being used by Central Empire, though the fact that the blanks available in circulation were not of a suitable diameter for these issues seems an equally likely reason for the virtual cessation of the practice of overstriking.

THE PRODUCTION OF THE COINAGE
The production of the large volume of bronze coinage issued by Carausius would have required manpower, technical expertise and a reasonable degree of administrative organisation. It is thus necessary to look in some detail at the methods of production likely to have been used.

Bronze is a fairly malleable metal and is one of the easier metals to strike into coin form. It is advantageous, though not absolutely necessary, to pre-heat the blanks before striking. The production of the coinage may be conveniently separated into two main processes, namely the production of the blank flans, and the actual striking of the design onto the flan.

By far the easiest method of obtaining a ready supply of blanks is to re-use, by overstriking, coins that are already in circulation. Such coins provide instant blanks with no extra work required, although the work-hardening caused by the initial striking will almost certainly require the blank to be heated before the second strike. The newly produced coin will often show traces of the original design on some parts of the flan. There is no doubt that overstriking of the existing coinage took place in the early years of the reign of Carausius when a rapid output of coinage was required. Many of these coins show signs of overstriking, often on coins originally issued under the Gallic Empire by Postumus, Victorinus and the *Tetrici*. Coins of the Central Empire, notably of Gallienus are also often utilised in this way. Such overstrikes occur on Carausian coins of the unmarked type, and also on coins exhibiting the *L, C* and *RSR* marks. This indicates an acceptability of the method of overstriking at all four centres of production.

Freshly produced blanks were also used by all the minting centres, though the metal used may well have often originated from earlier coins, removed from circulation, being melted down and then cast into flans of suitable mass and diameter for the new coinage.

The metrology of the bronze coinage, discussed in detail later in this chapter, indicates that rigorous weight standards were not employed. It is likely that the general aim of the administration in the early part of the reign was to produce coins with a mean mass of approximately 3.5 gms., but that a large degree of tolerance in the individual coin masses was allowable. This is exemplified by two coins from the same pair of dies found in the Penard and Little Orme I Hoards respectively. Boon (Boon 1974) regards these as "early, rough but orthodox productions". Their masses are 2.28 gms. and 9.55gms. and are thus from the extreme ends of the mass-range.

Blanks may be prepared by allowing the molten metal to flow into suitable circular recesses in clay. If this method is employed it will often leave spurs on the flans corresponding to the inter-recess channels. Such examples do exist for the Carausian bronze coinage, but are more the exception than the rule. An alternative method of blank preparation is to allow small droplets of molten metal to drop onto a flat cool surface allowing fairly rapid solidification into a globular flan shape. This method is quick and an experienced worker would be able to gauge flan sizes with a reasonable degree of accuracy. The globular effect would be easily flattened out in the striking process. It is likely that this method was predominantly used in the manufacture of blanks for the Carausian bronze coinage.

Much has been written concerning the metal content of late third century *antoniniani*. Cope (Cope 1974) analysed several antoniniani including some issued by Carausius, but there is an inherent danger in reading too much into such small percentages of silver in the coinage. Although the mint could, if it so desired, add corresponding amounts of silver to a melt with reasonable

accuracy, the coin using public would not possess the technology available to determine the exact fineness of so base a coinage. It seems more likely that the small traces of silver appearing in the coinage are by-products of earlier billon coins entering the melt prior to blank production.

There is little doubt that the bronze coinage of Carausius was issued in plentiful quantity. R.I.C. (Webb 1933) lists nearly one thousand varieties. It seems reasonable, for the purpose of order of magnitude calculations, to assume that on average each variety utilises about five reverse dies, (*PAX AVG* with olive branch and vertical sceptre probably exists in over two hundred die-forms). There are also many reverse varieties that have come to light in recent years, that are published or are awaiting publication elsewhere. The total number of reverse dies used on the coinage could thus be reasonably estimated at about ten thousand.

The average coin production possible from a single die has produced research notably from Sellwood and Stewart (Stewart 1963). In the light of this research it would seem reasonable to suppose that the average life-time yield of a Roman style reverse die may be of the order of ten thousand strikings. Some dies would undoubtedly last longer, whilst others may not be used to extinction or may develop die-flaws or break earlier. Thus as a rough order of magnitude calculation we should look at a total output of Carausian *antoniniani* as being in the region of anything up to 100 million *antoniniani*, giving the mass of coinage metal required as about 350 tonnes, taking an average coin to be about 3.5 grams.

The time and manpower required to produce such a coinage must be considered. Although the workmanship on the reverse dies is not, as a general rule, of the highest technical quality, each die would take some time to prepare. By using previously prepared punches an engraver could reasonably be expected to produce at least three reverse dies in a day. This makes the completion of the ten thousand or so dies postulated above a distinct possibility for a small team of engravers during a reign of approximately 2500 days.

The number of obverse dies used on the coinage is likely to be smaller, since the obverse die, normally held firmly in the block would be expected to have a much longer life-span (Stewart ibid). Artistically and technically, with very few exceptions, the obverse dies are of a much higher standard than the reverse dies, and would be expected to take correspondingly longer to produce. A most efficient way to produce these dies would be to use the method of hubbing. This method involves the careful carving of a prototype portrait onto a bronze base. This may be carved in relief as it will appear on the final coin, making the engravers task easier. When the engraver is satisfied with his efforts the punch so formed may be hardened by heat-treatment. The punch is then driven into the heated die giving the incuse version of the portrait that is required. (Brockages show a similar effect, often with great detail still present, the lower coin trapped in the dies, having cooled and hardened, acting in the same way as the hubbing punch.) The lettering may then be added to the die using normal lettering punches. One hub may thus produce many separate dies, each capable of producing many coins.

The two coins illustrated (Plate 3 Nos.7-10) share the same reverse die with the legend *ΓAETITIA AVG*, but the portraits which appear to be identical, are surrounded by lettering in different positions. The coins can not therefore come from the same obverse die, but do seem to originate from the same obverse die-hub. It would be easy at first glance to categorize either coin as barbarous, especially in the light of the mis-engraved reverse legend, but the fact that the production centre was sophisticated enough to employ hubbing makes it likely that the source was an official one, and even if this were not the case, it does illustrate beyond doubt that hubbing was a known technique in Britain at this time.

Many obverses exist where the portraits, or sometimes parts of the portraits, are so similar that hubbing is the most likely method of die production. Thus the production of the large number of obverse dies required for the coinage would pose little problem to a well organised but small band of hub/die engravers.

No evidence remains of the rates of striking coins achieved in Roman times, but there is written evidence of the workshop practice employed in the region of Afghanistan in relatively recent times for the hand-striking of coins (Sellwood in conversation 1994). A good striker is cited as producing up to thirty-five coins in one minute, with blanks being fed in by an assistant. Such work is physically demanding, but could be carried out on a fairly continuous basis by three teams working for ten minutes, then resting during a twenty minute recovery period.

If in Carausian times the production rate was as low as one coin every five seconds, or twelve per minute, in a ten hour day, allowing for change-overs and minor delays, such a set of workers could produce nearly seven thousand coins. During the length of the reign, allowing for occasional days off, a single team could be expected to produce about fifteen million coins.

It thus seems probable that the entire volume of bronze coinage postulated could be produced by a total workforce numbering not much more than one hundred people, distributed around the workshops in production.

The coinage attributed to the latter part of the reign is often of a higher technical standard, being struck on larger and better-formed flans. Many of these later coins retain traces of surface silvering, indicating a further process of leaching silver to the surface of the coin, in order to give it a silvered appearance on release from the mint. Feasible methods of producing this effect were well within the technical capabilities of the workshops at this time (Cope 1972).

THE METROLOGY OF THE UNMARKED ISSUES

For a study of the metrology of any coinage to be meaningful, several important factors require consideration. The sample size has to be as large as possible in order to iron out any random fluctuations. For this study the masses and diameters of over one thousand specimens of the unmarked coinage of Carausius were recorded. The mass of each specimen was recorded on an *Ohaus* portable balance to an accuracy of ±0.01 grams, and the diameter of each specimen was measured to an accuracy of ±1 millimetre using vernier callipers. This second measurement requires some elaboration since few Carausian coins possess regular circular flans. In order to overcome this problem when dealing with irregular flans, a mean of the longest and shortest diameters was taken.

The choice of samples in such a metrology is important. Museum collections built over a number of years often contain a predominance of well-struck, large-flanned specimens chosen to a certain extent on aesthetic grounds. Such collections do not present a true picture of the circulating coinage of the time, and to ensure valid results they should, in most cases, be eliminated from such studies, exception being made for complete excavation finds housed in some local museums. Corroded coins often put on a considerable amount of weight due to oxidation, and such specimens should be ignored, as should chipped, broken or pierced specimens which have obviously lost weight. Very worn specimens should also be rejected from such studies. All the above restrictions on choice of coin were taken into account in this survey. Also omitted from the survey were coins where there was some doubt as to their unmarked status, such as an exergue slightly off-flan.

In order to create as random a sample as possible, all unmarked coins, with the exception of those outlined above and any obvious barbarous copy, were taken from a wide selection of sites including *Abona*, Lydney, Packenham, Caerleon, Caerwent, Colchester, Cirencester, Chichester, Lincoln, London, Winchester, Aldborough, Chester, *Segontium*, Salisbury, *Verulamium*, Richborough, Silchester, Dinorben, Deganwy, York, *Magna* (Kenchester), Bath, Ilchester and Neatham.

The table (figure 7) shows the breakdown in terms of mass and diameter for one thousand and nine randomly selected, unmarked issues of Carausius.

A graph of numbers against mass was produced (figure 5). When a smooth curve is fitted, a significant dip appears in the number of coins with masses in the range 3.51-3.75 gms., giving the impression of a twin-peak in the mass distribution. The immediate temptation would be to interpret this as evidence for two different weight standards being in operation for the production of the

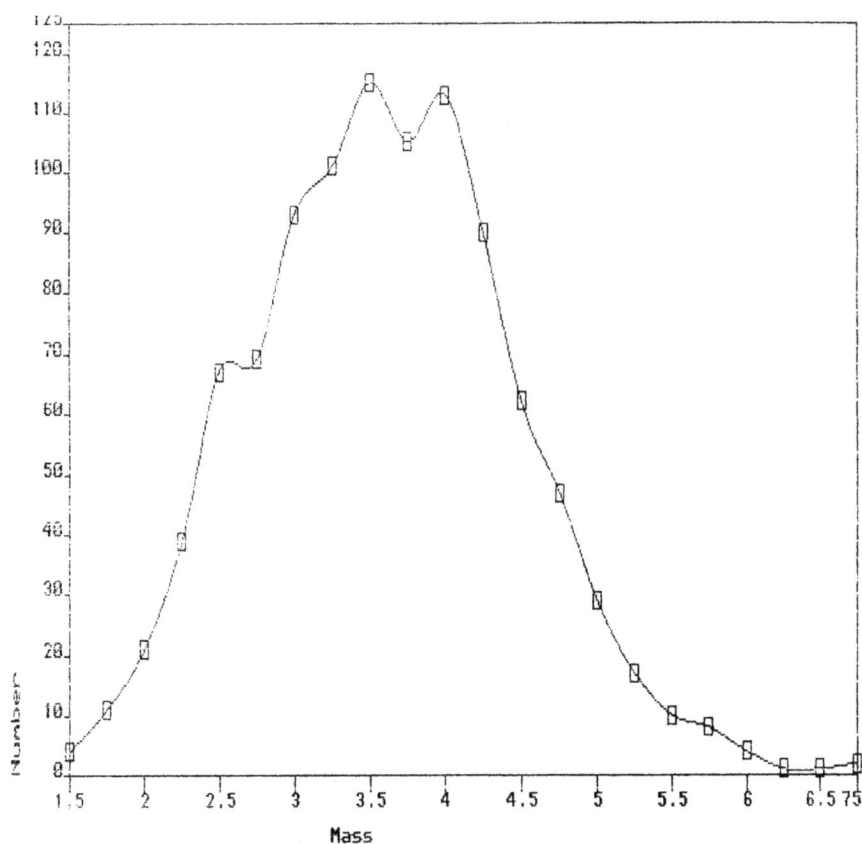

FIGURE 5 GRAPH OF THE METROLOGY OF THE UNMARKED BRONZE COINAGE

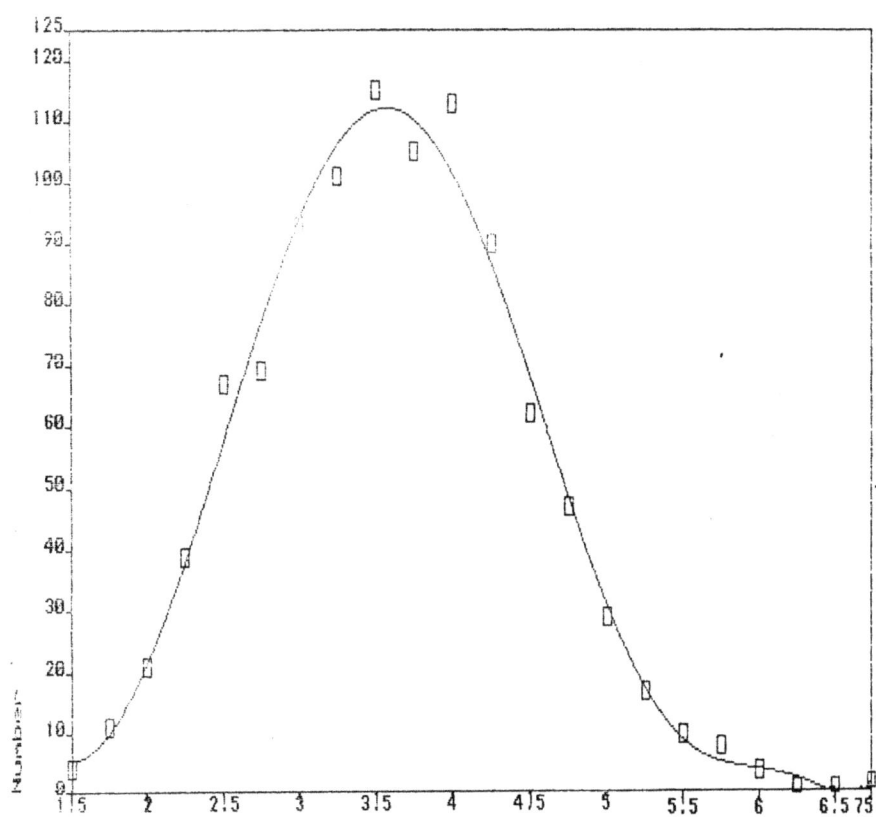

FIGURE 6 AS FIGURE 5, BUT FITTED TO A NORMAL DISTRIBUTION

25

Diameters in mm. less than/ equal to

gms.	17	19	21	23	25	27	TOTAL
1.50	2	2	0	0	0	0	4
1.75	4	5	2	0	0	0	11
2.00	3	10	6	2	0	0	21
2.25	6	18	14	1	0	0	39
2.50	3	20	33	8	3	0	67
2.75	5	23	33	7	1	0	69
3.00	2	30	46	14	1	0	93
3.25	4	23	56	11	7	0	101
3.50	2	25	64	19	5	0	115
3.75	2	21	39	34	7	2	105
4.00	1	18	47	30	17	0	113
4.25	1	11	37	32	6	3	90
4.50	0	7	22	25	8	0	62
4.75	0	3	24	14	5	1	47
5.00	0	2	7	13	6	1	29
5.25	0	2	1	9	5	0	17
5.50	0	1	4	4	1	0	10
5.75	0	0	3	4	1	0	8
6.00	0	1	0	2	1	0	4
6.25	0	0	1	0	0	0	1
6.50	0	0	0	0	0	1	1
6.75	0	0	0	2	0	0	2
TOTAL	35	222	439	231	74	8	1009

(Left margin label: M A S S)

FIGURE 7 TABLE SHOWING THE METROLOGY OF THE UNMARKED BRONZE COINAGE

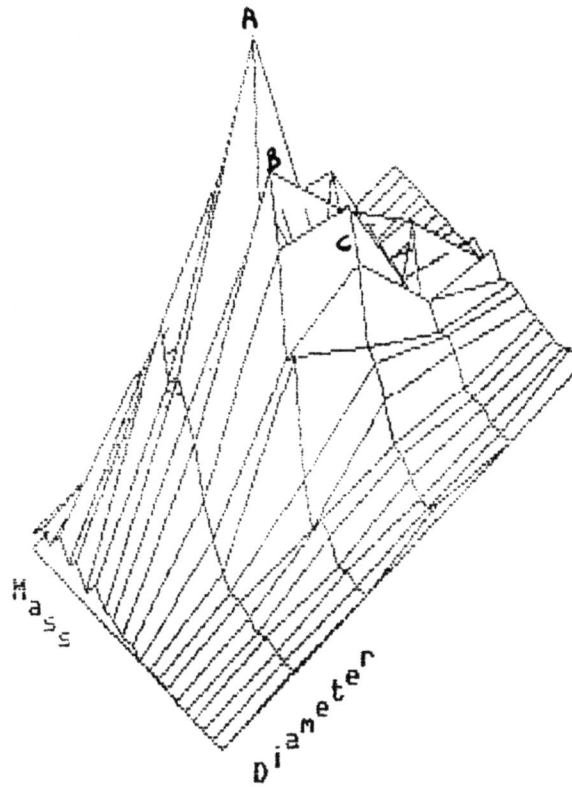

FIGURE 8 METROLOGY FITTED TO A THREE-DIMENSIONAL SURFACE

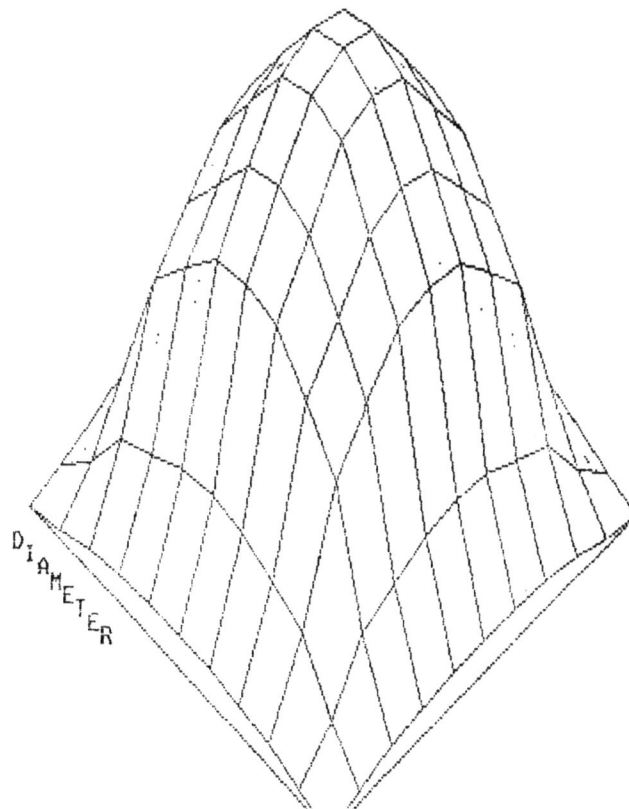

FIGURE 9 THREE-DIMENSIONAL SURFACE OF A NORMAL DISTRIBUTION

unmarked coinage during the reign, with the possibility of the heavier standard coinciding with the issue of the larger-flanned and better struck *antoniniani* at the *L* and *C* mints. The evidence is not, however, as clear cut as it may at first seem, since the second graph (figure 6), shows how a normal distribution curve fits the same points extremely well, allowing for only small variations in numbers. It would be dangerous to regard the evidence for two weight standards as being conclusive, but it does seem that a mean weight standard of about 3.6 gms, was aimed at by the issuing authorities. The Roman pound has a mass of approximately 327 gms (Webb 1933), so this would indicate a production rate of about ninety *antoniniani* to the pound.

The advent of computer-aided graphics has now made the production of three-dimensional surfaces readily available. Thus the number of coins, their masses and their diameters may now be illustrated on the same graph. An attempt has been made to use this capability (figure 8), in order to differentiate any separate mint practices that occurred during the issue of the unmarked coinage. An ideal single-standard issue should produce the normal-distribution surface shown below (figure 9). If two separate mint practices were operational, even if both used the same weight standard, it is possible that each may use slightly different flan-diameters, consequently producing coins on flans of differing thickness. Such a three-dimensional analysis would then yield a surface with two distinct peaks. The surface produced (figure 8) does seem to show three such peaks A, B and C which could possibly represent either the existence of three different workshops, or alternatively three distinct phases of coin production. It should be emphasised, once again, that extreme caution must be applied into avoiding reading too much into figures where a small change could radically affect the surface being generated.

This method of creating a surface in three-dimensions when analysing the metrology of a coinage is used here for the first time. Although the results are inconclusive due to the size of the available sample, the method may well prove itself to be a powerful one in distinguishing between the outputs of various *officinae* in other areas of ancient numismatics, enabling scholars to determine the contribution of each workshop to a coinage. It could prove most useful in the analysis of large hoards, where specimens are often in near mint-state, and have been all subjected to similar chemical conditions during burial.

Chapter Five

Coin Supply in Carausian Britain

The link between site finds derived from casual coin loss and coin supply to a site in a given period may at first seem obvious. An elementary approach would be merely to count the number of coins from any chosen period and relate that number to the total site yield. This would, however, require a stable currency system with standard denominations being supplied in a constant ratio. The actual monetary value of a coin will often determine how hard any loser tries to recover it, so that the ratio of high value coins to low value coins found on a site is unlikely to be in the same ratio at which they would have been found in circulation.

One great advantage of the study of Third Century site finds is that the antoninianus was the only denomination to circulate extensively, and this eliminates the complication mentioned above.

In 1963, Alison Ravetz (Ravetz 1963), produced a formula that took into account another important factor, namely the length of the period of issue of any given type of coin find. This expressed all coin finds from a site on a single numerical basis from which a histogram representing finds from a given period could be produced.

$$\text{Ravetz Number} = \frac{\text{coins per period} \times 1000}{\text{period length} \times \text{site total}}$$

Whereas this formula will give a good indication of relative coin supply provided that the currency is stable, it does not take into account the lifetime in circulation of the various issues. This is particularly important in the last quarter of the Third Century.

A minor complication exists due to Gresham's Law, In every country where two kinds of legal money exist in circulation, the bad money always drives out the good, and during this period some of the coinage was of very low quality and little intrinsic value. In addition there is also the question of how, if at all, Aurelian's reform of the antoninianus may have affected Britain, although the supply of Aurelianic coin to Britain was so minimal that any effect would be unlikely to manifest itself. The large issues of barbarous radiates in the second half of the third century could be included in any relevant calculations, but as these must be classed as unofficial issues, it will clarify the picture to remove them from the initial calculations.

A most important complication towards the end of the third century, is the lifetime spent by any particular type of coin in circulation. Since a coin can only become a casual loss if it is still in active circulation then an issue with a circulation lifetime of fifty years will be ten times

more likely to be lost, and subsequently found, all other factors remaining constant, than an issue having a five year span. If the assumption is made that recoinage involving the demonetisation of the antoninianus occurred almost immediately after the overthrow of Allectus in AD 296, then we have a fixed terminus ante quem on which to base calculations. We know from the Blackmoor Hoard (Bland 1982) that at this stage the coinage issued under the Gallic Empire was still in active circulation. Thus a typical Gallic coin could have been in circulation for nearly thirty years before the recoinage, while one of Carausius would not have circulated for more than ten years, and some late issues of Allectus might have circulated for less than a year.

As a first approximation it would be reasonable to assume that an average Gallic Empire coin may have typically enjoyed thirty year circulation period, compared with maybe fifteen years for an Aurelianic coin, whereas an average British Empire coin may only have spent a maximum of five years in circulation. Thus an examination of casual losses on a site would show an imbalance of the ratio 30:15:5 or 6:3:1 in the numbers of specimens found from the three groups, Gallic Empire coins being six times as likely, and Aurelianic coins three times as likely as British Empire coins, to be lost on the site, providing of course that the population and monetary habits of the site do not change too radically over the period in question. Thus, if we are to use site finds from the three groups as a basis for the calculation of coin supply, then they must be adjusted by the above ratio.

In order to create a more realistic picture of coin supply another factor has to be taken into account. Coins enter circulation only during their issue period, and one assumes that they can be lost at any time during their life-span from their initial day of issue, but the rate of coin loss of any issue should be proportional to the number actually in circulation at that time. Since this number increases during the reign, but is always decreasing after its final issue is complete, calculus has to be employed in order to create a meaningful picture.

An assumption that needs to be made is that coins are supplied during the period of issue at an average rate k. The constant of proportionality, which may be described as the loss constant, is symbolised by Ø. The average supply of coinage is assumed to continue for t_1, the length of the issue period.

During the period of supply, a 1st order differential equation will give the rate at which the number of coins in circulation changes.

$$\frac{dN}{dt} = k - \emptyset N \tag{1}$$

Where N represents the number of coins of that issue in circulation at any given time during that period. This equation may be solved as follows to give the number of coins still present in circulation at the end of the period of issue.

$$\int_0^{N_r} \frac{dN}{(k - \emptyset N)} = \int_0^{t_1} dt \tag{2}$$

where Nr is the number of coins remaining in circulation at the end of the period.

Integrating....

$$\text{Log}_e \left(\frac{k - \emptyset Nr}{k} \right) = -\emptyset t_1 \tag{3}$$

thus

$$k - \emptyset Nr = k.e^{-\emptyset t_1} \tag{4}$$

and

$$Nr = \frac{k}{\emptyset} (1 - e^{-\emptyset t_1}) \tag{5}$$

This gives Nr , the number of coins remaining in circulation at the end of the reign . Thus the number of coins lost during the reign is given by subtracting the number remaining from the total number produced, kt. Thus number lost = N_L , where ..

$$N_L = k \left(t_1 - \frac{(1 - e^{-\emptyset t_1})}{\emptyset} \right) \tag{6}$$

At the end of the supply period no further coins enter circulation, but coins continue to be lost at a rate proportional to the number remaining in circulation.

Thus the rate at which coins are lost from circulation after supply ceases is given by..

Number lost per year if there is no continued input = $\frac{dN}{dt}$

where $\frac{dN}{dt} = -\emptyset N$ (7)

Where $\emptyset$ is the same loss constant as previously considered.

Solving this equation..

$$\int_{N_r}^{N} \frac{dN}{N} = -\emptyset \int_0^{t_2} dt \tag{8}$$

Where N is the number of coins still in circulation a time t_2 after the end of the issue period, and Nr is the number of coins still in circulation at the end of the issue period. This loss rate will only apply until the end of the circulation period of the issue concerned. Thus in practice t_2 is the lifetime of the issue in circulation after supply ceases.

Thus

$$\log_e \left(\frac{N}{Nr} \right) = -\emptyset t_2 \tag{9}$$

Thus the number of coins lost between the end of the issue period and the end of the circulation period is...

$$Nm = Nr (1 - e^{-\emptyset t_2}) \tag{10}$$

The total number lost, N_T will thus be the sum of equations (6) and (10).

$$\text{Total number lost} = N_T = N_M + N_L \tag{11}$$

so

$$N_T = Nr (1 - e^{-\emptyset t_2}) + \emptyset \left(t_1 - \frac{(1 - e^{-\emptyset t_1})}{\emptyset} \right)$$

substituting for Nr , it follows that...

$$N_T = \frac{k}{\emptyset} \left(e^{-\emptyset(t_1 + t_2)} - e^{-\emptyset t_2} + \emptyset t_1 \right) \tag{12}$$

If we let

$$t_1 + t_2 = t_a$$

and

$$t_2 = t_b$$

and

$$t_1 = t_c$$

then..

$$N_T = \frac{k}{\emptyset} \left(e^{-\emptyset t_a} - e^{-\emptyset t_b} + \emptyset t_c \right) \tag{13}$$

rearranging.. ($\emptyset$ being a constant)....

$$k = \frac{\emptyset N_T}{\left(e^{-\emptyset t_a} - e^{-\emptyset t_b} + \emptyset t_c \right)} \tag{14}$$

On a site where casual losses are recovered, and any trends are not disguised by hoard material, it is reasonable that the number of finds, N_F will be directly proportional to the total number of losses, N_T.

k will thus give us a comparative number indicating the rate of coin supply in the given issue period. Thus..

$$k \text{ is proportional to } A.N_F \tag{15}$$

Where N_F is the total number of finds on the site from the issue period , and A is a complex constant detailed below.

$$A = \emptyset \left(e^{-\emptyset t_a} - e^{-\emptyset t_b} + \emptyset t_c \right)^{-1}$$

where

ta = time from beginning of supply to end of circulation period.

tb = time from end of supply to end of circulation period,

and

t_c = length of supply period (usually length of the reign).

The constant Ø, is a measure of the fraction of the coins in circulation lost in a given year, and has to be estimated. k figures may be calculated for different values of Ø, such as 0.01 (1%) , 0.02 (2%) or 0.005 («%), and results compared. The value of A may then be calculated, and multiplying the number of finds from the given issue period by A will give a relative value for the rate of coin supply during the period in question.

An undoubted advantage of such a method is that it may be applied to a period such as the Gallic Empire, or also to the issues of single emperors. If some figures are supplied, and a loss rate of 1% is assumed , the following table may be completed....

Period	Dates	t_a	t_b	t_c	Ø	A
Gallic	259-73	38	24	14	0.01	27
Aurelianic	273-86	24	11	13	0.01	48
British	286-96	11	1	10	0.01	166

The model here is simplified to the extent that the table is based on whole years. An assumption is also made that after the recoinage of A.D.296, the end of normal circulation for the *antoninianus* in Britain is conjectured at A.D.297, the bulk of remaining coins disappearing quickly from circulation, a trend that hoard evidence strongly supports.

In order to convert the histograms constructed from the Ravetz formula ...

$$\text{Period value} = \frac{\text{coins per period}}{\text{length of period}} \times \frac{1000}{\text{site total}}$$

it is first necessary to work out the relative effect that this formula has on each period, which for a given set of coin data is simply proportional to the length of the period. This factor will be referred to as B.

The ratio A/B will give a factor that will convert the height of each bar of the old style histogram to the new form. This ratio may then be normalised to the Gallic Empire issues for direct comparison purposes.

Period	A	B	A/B	Normalised
Gallic	27	71.	0.38	1.00
Aurelianic	47	100	0.47	1.24
British	166	77	2.15	5.66

Thus a histogram representing the actual supply of coins into circulation in each period may be constructed by the following steps....

 a) Leave the Gallic Empire bar on the original coin-loss histogram at its original height.
 b) Increase the height of the Aurelianic bar by a factor of 1.24.
 c) Increase the height of the Carausian bar by a factor of 5.66.

The same calculations may be performed for estimated rates of loss for 2% and 0.5%, with the following results, which are again normalised to the Gallic Empire figure.

This table represents the factor by which the height of each histogram bar, (originally signifying the number of coins found from that period), must be multiplied in order to construct a more realistic representation of coin supply to that location.

Period	Loss Rate 2%	Loss Rate 1%	Loss Rate 0.5%
Gallic	1.00	1.00	1.00
Aurelianic	1.20	1.24	1.17
British	5.14	5.66	9.20

The loss rates chosen above would seem reasonable. They assume that anything between one in fifty and one in two-hundred coins are casually lost per annum. The histograms shown illustrate the effect when losses from several well-documented sites are studied. These charts are all based on a 1% per annum rate of coin loss. It should be noted that a smaller rate of loss would accentuate the effect on the British Empire bar.

The striped bars shown to the fore represent the coin finds from each site based on the Ravetz formula. The filled-in bars behind represent the coin supply in each period produced by the formula derived above, and normalised to the Gallic Empire bar on the former representation.

It can be seen immediately that the supply of coinage to the British sites chosen was substantial. In the case of major sites in the south of the country this rate of supply of coinage is shown to be greater than during the Gallic Empire period. While northern sites, especially those near the Wall show a supply rate that is lower than under the Gallic Empire. This can be used as numerical evidence for the reduction in military presence in the Wall area at that time.

The almost total lack of supply of coinage to Britain in the Aurelianic period is most marked. The figures used in the calculations do not include Barbarous Radiate types, and if, as seems likely, their production was most prevalent in the early 280s, then their supply would certainly have met a required demand.

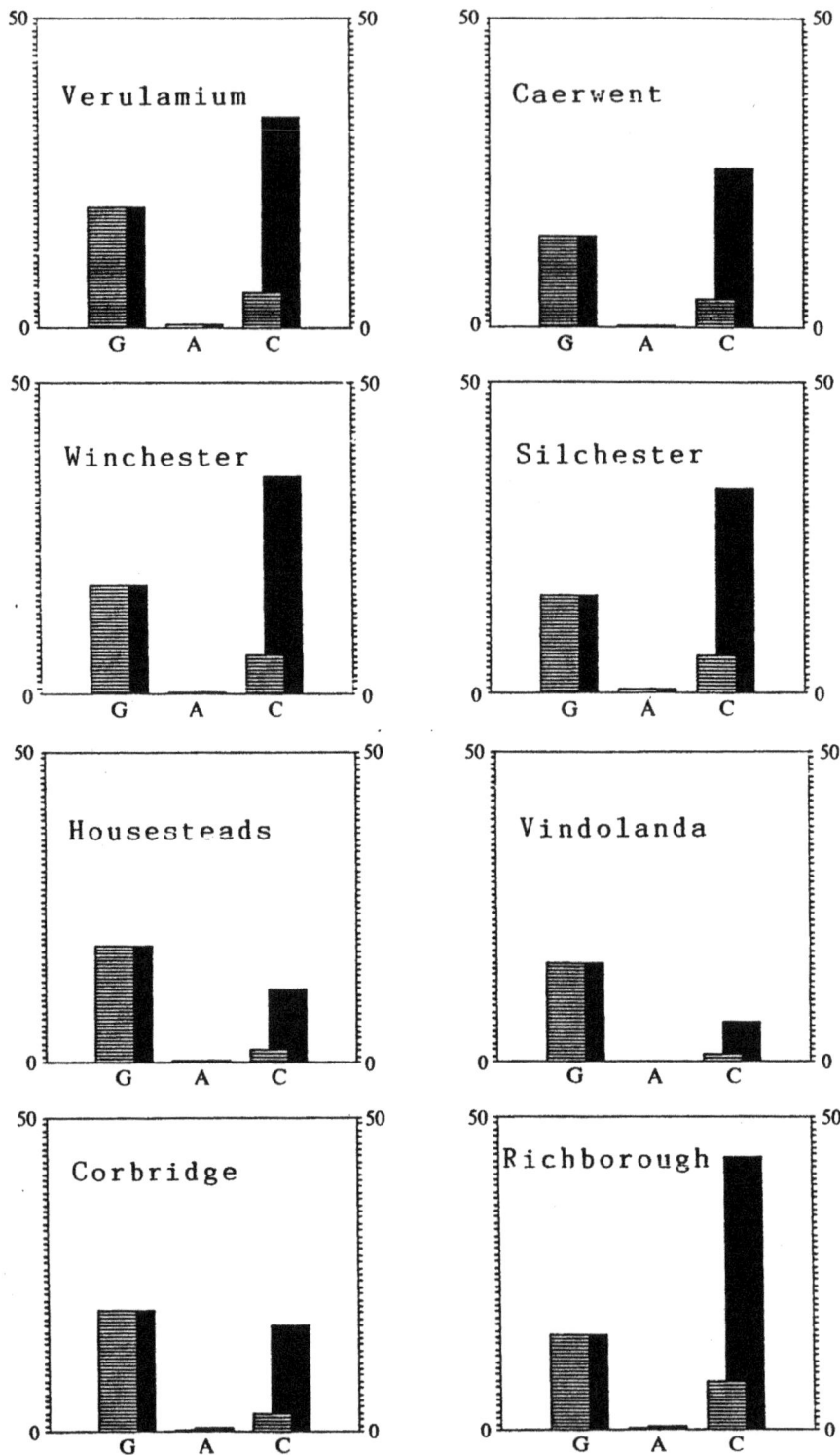

Histograms representing actual supply of coins into circulation in Britain in late-third century at selected sites: **Verulamium**, after R. Reece, 'The coins', in *Verulamium Excavations* (ed. S. Frere), vol. III (Oxford, 1984); **Winchester**, figures courtesy of Winchester Research Unit for Archaeology and personal inspection of the material; **Caerwent**, **Housesteads**, **Corbridge**, after P. J. Casey, *Roman Coinage in Britain* (Aylesbury, 1980), p. 30 (Caerwent), p. 51 (Housesteads), p. 31 (Corbridge); **Silchester**, after G. C. Boon, *The Coins of Silchester* (Reading Museum, Unpublished Catalogue, 1954); **Vindolanda**, after R. J. Brickstock, *Fel. Temp. Reparatio Copies*, B.A.R. 176 (Oxford, 1987), pp. 289–90; **Richborough**, after R. Reece, *The Roman Coins of Richborough*, Institute of Archaeology, Bulletin No. 18 (London, 1981), pp. 49–71. ▤, Ravetz formula; ■, my formula.

FIGURE 10 COIN SUPPLY TO EIGHT MAJOR SITES

In conclusion, the figures make it likely that the overall rate of supply of coinage to Britain under the British Empire was greater than that under the Gallic Empire. Carausius and Allectus needed to pay their troops, and any supply of coinage from the continent would have been negligible. Allowing for inflation which was present at the end of the third Century, more coinage would have been required than under the Gallic Empire for a given number of troops. The possibility that the number of personnel on the military pay-roll had increased also exists, since in addition to the Roman Fleet, any supporters that had joined Carausius on the continent would have come over to Britain with the initial invasion party, further increasing the numbers on the pay-roll.

Whereas the Ravetz Formula gives a good guide to coinage supply within the framework of a stable and continuing currency, the coinage reform of 294-296 A.D., not implemented in Britain until immediately after the defeat of Allectus, and the subsequent demonetisation of the antoninianus requires the new method outlined above in order to create a clearer picture of the coinage supply.

Chapter Six

The Chronology of the Coinage

The marked issues of Carausius exhibit a complex series of index marks. These form a pattern which should enable the marked coinage to be placed in chronological order. The unmarked coinage was issued alongside these marked issues and a clear overall view of the coinage is necessary in order to place the unmarked issues in the correct context.

The problem of placing the unmarked coins in context was first looked at by Webb (Webb 1907). In this work he laid down a possible sequence of the marked issues, but postulated that the unmarked issues were mostly early productions from the L mint which preceded the marked issues, though a few, on stylistic grounds, he suggested may have emanated from the early days of the C mint. Webb adjusted his ideas slightly as a result of the discovery of the Linchmere Hoard (Webb 1925), and this, with little further modification, forms the basis of the system of sequence marks that is published in *Roman Imperial Coinage, Volume V(ii)* (Webb 1933).

Although the system of sequence-marking would be considerably simplified by considering all unmarked issues to be early, this is unlikely to be the case. Some of the issues undoubtedly come from the early part of the reign, and may well precede the initial issues from the L and C mints, but it also likely that the unmarked issues continued well into the reign. King has pointed out (King 1984), that the "moustached" portrait used on some the unmarked coins is very similar in style to that used at the C mint in conjunction with the issues bearing index marks *CXXI* and *MCXXI*, which Webb (Webb *ibid*), and Carson (Carson 1971) both place towards the middle period of the reign.

Bland (Bland 1982) also suggests that the unmarked issues were produced until well into the reign, on the basis that although Linchmere contains a mere 6% of unmarked issues, leading to the inevitable suggestion that such coins were both out of fashion and production by the latter half of the reign, the Blackmoor Hoard, buried at the end of the reign of Allectus, contains 57% unmarked issues in a total of 436 coins of Carausius.

The unmarked coinage is extremely prolific. Styles vary considerably and it is likely that some of the obviously hastily produced issues of crude style belong to very early in the reign. These would have been struck in the early days of the regime, possibly before Carausius, himself, came over to Britain. It is worth noting at this point that the *Adventvs* types from the unmarked mint (Plate 2 Nos.7-9) are very similar in style and quality to the *Adventvs* types of the L, C, and RSR mints, and were, in all probability, issued at the time of Carausius's official arrival in Britain.

Many of the unmarked issues appear to be of a style less accomplished than this issue and are probably earlier. This supports the likelihood that the unmarked 'mint' was in production before the other three mints opened.

The order of sequence-marks set out by Webb was modified by Carson (Carson 1959 and Carson 1971). Carson's proposed order for the issues of the L and C mints is sound and complies well with hoard evidence. The dates of the issues bearing other index marks do, however, in the light of recent hoard evidence need careful reconsideration.

Both Carson and Webb dated the 'Rouen' issues towards the end of the reign. Carson based this premise on his assumption that the legend beginning *IMPCCARAVSIVS...* was introduced some time after 291. The Little Orme I hoard of 1907 (Seaby 1956), contained two of these coins, whilst the latest marked issues were marked *F/O/ML* and *MCXXI* respectively. It is inconceivable that the large later issues of the reign are not represented whilst two extremely late issues, in Carson's view, from Rouen find inclusion in the hoard. Two extremely large hoards, both containing a mere handful of Carausian coins have come to light in recent years. The hoard from Normanby in 1985 (Bland and Burnett 1988) contained nearly 48,000 coins ending with 73 of Carausius terminating in one example of *F/O/ML* and one of *F/O/C*. This hoard significantly contained one coin of the Rouen mint. The Dorchester Hoard (King forthcoming), contained over 10,000 coins ending with 72 of Carausius terminating in one piece sequence-marked *ML*. This contained three Rouen coins. The Croydon Hoard, skilfully reconstituted by Burnett (Burnett and Casey 1984), which also terminates with the mark *ML* also contains a single Rouen Coin. This evidence leaves little doubt that the Rouen mint was operational at the very beginning of the reign, in all likelihood commencing when Carausius assumed the purple, probably at Rouen. This early dating of the Rouen mint is suggested by Burnett and Casey (*ibid*), who state that " *In our view, however, the inclusion of C(aesar) in the titles at Rouen is irrelevant...... It seems clear, then, that C was used at Rouen well before it was added in Britain.*"

These issues have been successfully ascribed to Rouen (Huvelin and Loriot 1983), although Giard has made efforts to ascribe them elsewhere (Giard 1995) with reference to a coin bearing an armed bust left found at Jublains having a reverse of similar style to one struck at Lyons (a similar obverse on a coin found at Chantilly is illustrated (Plate 3 Nos.1-2)). A second article by Huvelin (Huvelin forthcoming) now seems to reinforce the

	L	C	Unmark	Rouen	RSR	Other
Oct286-Mar287				R, OPR, none		
Mar287-Oct287	ML	C C/ /			RSR	BRI, V/*/
Oct287-Mar288	ML	C C/ /				
Mar288-Oct288	L_ ML	MC				
Oct288-Mar289	F_O ML	F_O C				
Mar289-Oct289	F_O ML	MSC,SMC MSCC				
Oct289-Mar290	F_O ML	CXXI				
Mar290-Oct290	B_E MLXXI	MCXXI				
Oct290-Mar291	B_E MLXXI	S_C C	S_C			
Mar291-Oct291	S_P MLXXI	S_P C	S_P			
Oct291-Mar292	S_P MLXXI	S_P C	S_P			
Mar292-Oct292	S_P MLXXI	S_P C	S_P			
Oct292-Mar293	S_P ML	SPC	S_P			

FIGURE 11 TABLE OF SEQUENCE MARKS ACCORDING TO WILLIAMS (1996)

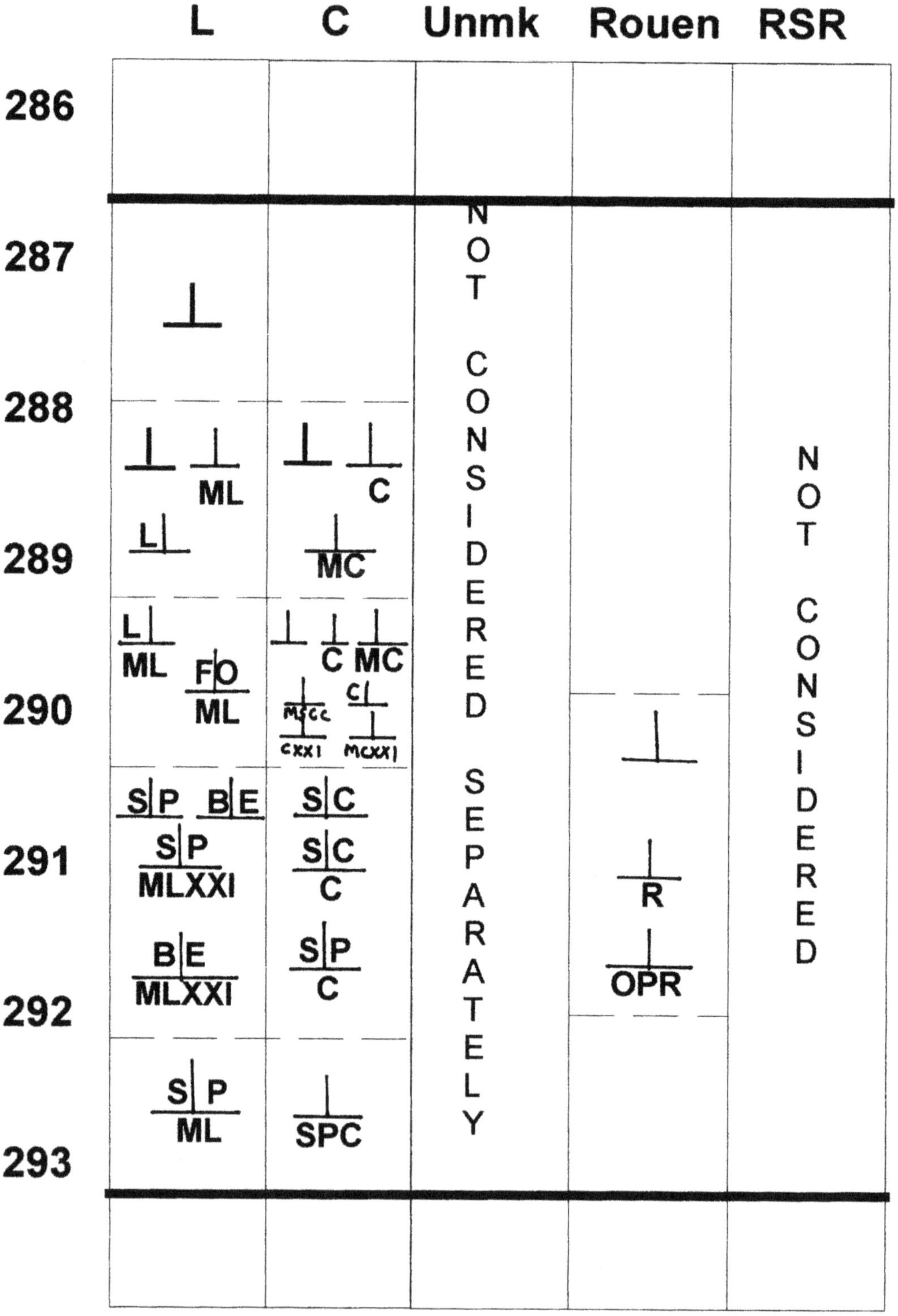

FIGURE 12 TABLE OF SEQUENCE MARKS ACCORDING TO WEBB (1925)

location of the mint to Rouen. The Rouen issues are relatively scarce, pointing to a short lived operation of the mint. Rouen coins do, however, emerge as site finds all over Southern Britain (see map under chapter on Mint Locations). Despite their markedly different style they are sometimes misdescribed as being issues of the London mint.

Carson also dated the *RSR* issues to the middle of the reign. The presence of *RSR* issues in the Normanby hoard (3), Croydon hoard (1) and the Dorchester hoard (1), now yields firm evidence that the *RSR* issues are early. Again it is almost certain that the *Adventvs* issues from this mint are contemporary with those of the *L*, *C* and unmarked mints. The output of this mint is again limited, especially of the bronze coinage, where the reverse type most common at other mints *viz. PAX AVG* has only been noted once during this study (Plate 3 Nos.5-6).

The early dating of the *RSR* mint has an important consequence, in that it was the major mint responsible for producing the fine silver *denarii*, though these coins do also occur from the other three 'mints' and again it is likely that the issues are contemporary.

Fine silver issues from all but the *RSR* mint are extremely scarce. At the *L* mint only the mark *ML* is recorded and at the *C* mint only the mark *C*, (King 1987). Unmarked issues also exist. Many of the reverse types used also echo the likelihood of the fine silver issue being early, such as *Adventvs* and *Expectate Veni* types (Plate 2 Nos.7,8 and 10) for both the *RSR* and unmarked mints. It may also be worth noting at this point that the only legion so far recorded on the fine silver coinage is the Fourth *Flavia* Legion (Plate 5 Nos.5 and 14b). The possibility is considered elsewhere that a detachment from this legion could have been entrusted with security at the minting centre(s). although the main part of this legion was, in whatever form it still existed, in all likelihood on the continent under Central Empire control, probably in Dacia (Webster1969).

The scarce *BRI* and *V/*/*/ coins (Plate 3 Nos.3-4) share a very similar obverse style. Both types seem early on these stylistic grounds and have certain similarities to the *RSR* coins, thus all three issues may well be considered contemporary.

As has been already mentioned, the unmarked coinage incorporates a great range of styles. The rough early coins seem to be superseded by styles akin to the early productions from the other mints, and then to progress further towards the high degree of competence exhibited by the later *F/O/ML* and *B/E/MLXXI* issues. It thus seems likely that the unmarked issues were produced until at least the second half of the reign.

Later coins from the *L* and *C* mints often have the letters *S P* or *S C* in the field. The exact meaning of these letters is far from understood. Suggestions have been put forward by Stukeley (Stukeley 1757) of *Sacra Pecvnia* and *Secvritas Perpetuae* but these are no more than mere conjecture. Webb (Webb 1907) thinks that they may relate to *officinae* indexing. Use of the letter *P* for *Prima* is acceptable, but what of *C*? The riddle is not, as yet, answered with any satisfaction.

Many of these *SP* and *SC* coins have unmarked exergues. They are all of comparable style to those *SP* and *SC* coins issued at the *L* and *C* mints and the strong possibility must exist that they are the later issues of the unmarked mint. If so, then it is likely that the unmarked mint remained in production throughout the reign of Carausius, but was closed on the accession of Allectus.

These new considerations may be used to modify the system set out by Carson (Carson 1971). The index marks were changed at intervals. It is unlikely that these intervals were random and it is probable that the marks changed at well regulated times. If, however, these changes occurred at annual intervals then there would be far more major issues than the brief span of Carausius's reign would allow. It is therefore worth considering a bi-annual review of index marks by each mint.

If, as seems probable, Carausius assumed the purple at Rouen between September and November 286, and began issuing coins immediately, then the start of each successive regnal year would make a most suitable point for mint practice to issue a new set of index marks. The second fixed date would then possibly be six months from this time, possibly about March or April. Alternatively, if Carausius did not come to Britain until early 287, or the British mints issuing as *L*, *C* and *RSR* were not inaugurated until this time, then either of these events could form the basis for a second anniversary-based change of index. It is thus felt worthwhile to examine the possibility of changes of index mark having taken place on a twice-yearly basis.

There are dangers in considering the time-span of an issue to be solely dependent on the relative abundance of surviving coins. It is quite possible that the mints were more active at certain points in the reign, notably at the outset. When the Carausian regime had become established, however, it is also likely that the need for coinage became much more stable.

Another complication may arise if for any reason the index mark were not changed but held over for a second term. The two prolific issues from the *L* mint, namely *F/O/ML* and *S/P/MLXXI* may well fall into this category.

A possible sequence of index marks has drawn up giving an updated chronology for the issues of the reign of Carausius. This is based upon hoard evidence, (see chapter on Hoards), and takes into account the possibility of a bi-annual change of index marks being a possibility at the mints. This new chronology is shown here, and is compared with the earlier versions of both Webb and Carson.

	L	C	Unmk	Rouen	RSR
286					
287	$\frac{\perp}{ML}$	$\frac{\perp}{C}$			
288	$\frac{L\vert}{ML}$	$\frac{\perp}{MC}$			
289	$\frac{F\vert O}{ML}$	$\frac{\perp}{SMC}$			$\frac{\perp}{RSR}$
290		$\overline{CXXI}$	I S S U E D		
291	$\frac{B\vert E}{MLXXI}$	$\frac{\perp}{MCXXI}$ $\frac{S\vert C}{C}$ $S\vert C$ $S\vert P$	T H R O U G H O U T		
292	$\frac{S\vert P}{MLXXI}$	$\frac{S\vert P}{C}$	R E I G N	$\frac{\perp}{R}$	
293	$\frac{S\vert P}{ML}$			$\frac{R}{OPR}$	

FIGURE 13 TABLE OF SEQUENCE MARKS ACCORDING TO CARSON (1971)

Stylistic trends have also played a major part in developing this chronology, as have the relative abundance of the types concerned, though this latter consideration has to be treated with some care in keeping with the comments above.

Certainly this scheme seems to fit in well with both the hoard evidence, and, though a certain degree of subjectivity has to be involved in any such judgements, with the style of virtually all the coins studied.

The concept of the coins bearing the marks *S C* and *S P* in the field, but no exergual index, being the successors from the 'unmarked' mint of the earlier completely unmarked coinage is particularly appealing. It also goes some way to explaining why completely unmarked coins exist in styles ranging from obviously early, crude and on small flans, through to issues of the later technically superior style on large well-formed flans. The changeover to coins bearing the aforesaid marks in the field coming after this style had been introduced. Coins bearing the field marks are without exception, ignoring the few obviously barbarous unofficial copies, struck with a good degree of technical competence on the larger flans.

Chapter Seven

The Location of the Mints

The actual location of the Carausian mints has, for a long time, posed a major problem to British numismatists. Coins of the continental style, now attributed to Rouen, form one group, but it is the Carausian coinage struck in Britain that forms the bulk of the finds.

Ignoring the more unusual index marks, which are dealt with later in this chapter, the British coinage divides into three main groups. These are, those marked *L* in the exergue, or very occasionally in the field, often in combination with other letters; those marked *C*, again often in combination; and those many coins bearing no index mark in the exergue, i.e. the unmarked coinage. A further group of coins, namely those bearing no exergual mark, but the letters *S/C* or *S/P* in the field also requires further consideration. These are discussed in the preceding chapter dealing with the chronology of the index marks.

Numismatists have, over the years, interpreted the marks in several different ways. Stukeley (Stukeley 1757) suggested that the *L* coins were issued by a mint situated in London, whilst the *C* coins were struck at *Cataractonium* or Catterick in Yorkshire. He also suggested that those coins bearing the mark *MC* were the product of a further mint situated in St.Davids in Dyfed, Stukeley's supposed birthplace of Carausius. In his uniquely eccentric way, Stukeley not only informs the reader of where these coins were struck, but also the actual date, if not the exact time of striking.

By the time of the publication of Webb's comprehensive work (Webb 1907) the concept of the *L* coins having been struck in London was widely accepted, but opinion was divided as to the location of the *C* mint between *Camulodunum* and *Clausentum*, present-day Bitterne on Southampton Water. Webb favoured the former, but accepted that arguments existed in favour of the latter.

Burnett (Burnett and Casey 1984) has made the point that some coins of Allectus have the index mark *CL* (Plate 6 Nos.17-18), stating that it would thus be more logical if the mint location were to either begin with these two letters, or else have its first two syllables beginning with these letters. He also mooted the possibility of *C* and *G* being non-differentiable to some engravers, thus opening possibilities for *Glevvm* or Gloucester, for example. If the lettering were interpreted in this way then *Calleva* could also re-emerge as a possible candidate.

A more unorthodox possibility was put forward by Bailey (Bailey 1981). He suggested that the letters *C* or *CL* could stand for *Classiensis* and that this may represent a Fleet Coinage. The obvious follow-on from this hypothesis, is that *L* would then represent *Legionensis* and that this coinage would provide for the army's pecuniary needs. Bailey suggests that Portchester would be a likely location for the mint issuing the *C* coinage, and that the fort may well have housed the headquarters of the fleet.

A further suggestion, based on Burnett's interpretation of the *C* or *G* indetermination, explores the possibility that the letters may represent *Gesoriacum,* (Boulogne), or even *Gallia,* (Morris 1986).

The unmarked coinage presents a more complex problem, since there are no letters present that may help locate the minting centre. Possibilities put forward have ranged from it being an early coinage of the London mint to Carson's suggestion that it was the product of a mint in Boulogne, (Carson 1971).

The key to an understanding of these index marks lies with an interpretation of the *C* mark. All possibilities should be re-evaluated in the light of current knowledge and site-finds. Details were compiled of the Carausian coin finds from eleven major sites yielding substantial numbers of coins. There is a need to treat the Carausian evidence in a separate way from that of Allectus, as the unmarked issues do not continue into that reign. Tables were then compiled showing the relative abundance of the various issues.

With the exception of Catterick, where the details of the coins were kindly provided by Mr. P. J.Casey, and Cirencester, where details of some seventy Carausian coins found in recent excavations were kindly provided by Dr. C. E. King, all the coins were examined personally, and several criteria were used in order to ensure a representative sample from each site. These are outlined below, and the tables appear on the following pages.

The exergual mark is the key feature on each coin in the survey. In many cases, owing to the irregular nature of the flan, this mark does not appear on the coin. Such coins were eliminated from the survey, although in many cases they had been, in the initial cataloguing, assigned such a mark often on the subjective basis of style. Very worn or corroded coins are notoriously difficult to catalogue fully, and such coins, where doubt as to the presence of a mark existed were also excluded.

Evidence of the coinage found in Colchester is of high importance in view of that city's claim as a minting centre, but the Colchester coins present some other difficulties. Whereas the coins from the recent excavations are well documented, Carausian coins are low in number (Reece *et al*. 1987). The coins in Colchester Museum, however, are much more plentiful, but represent accessions gathered over many years. Some have sound provenances and should therefore be included, whilst others are not guaranteed to have been found in the area, and must therefore be excluded. These factors, and those outlined above, have been taken into account in an effort to make the sample as representative as possible.

Any such statistical table must be produced with the *caveat* that low numbers of coins may provide a distorted picture, but nevertheless they should not be totally disregarded. The survey involved 1582 coins of Carausius, from the sites which were widely spread around the country. The totals in each category yield a sufficiently large total to produce an overall picture of the relative abundance of each type of index mark .

The picture created is that the unmarked issues constitute just over half the coinage; almost 60% if the *S/P* and *S/C* issues are included, whilst the *L* issues at just under 30% are almost three times as prolific as those bearing the *C* marks.

A second table (figure 15) normalises the totals to those of the *L* issues, giving a direct comparison of the relative abundance of the other issues at the respective sites. The tables are arranged in order of increasing relative abundance of *C* index-marked coins. Each of the possibilities for the location of the *C* mint can thus be examined in further detail.

Undoubtedly, the Colonia at Colchester was a centre of major importance in Roman Britain, though the high profile that it enjoyed in the first century had probably waned somewhat by the last quarter of the third century (Hull 1958). The ratio of British Empire : Gallic Empire site finds at Colchester is low (at 0.24), though on a par with the Tribal Capitals at Winchester and Canterbury.

Much of the enthusiasm for regarding Colchester as the site of the *C* mint derives from the publication of the famous Colchester Hoard, (Baldwin 1930), which was recorded as containing an unusually large number of such coins. Seventy eight out of a total of two hundred and seventy one coins of the British Empire, (29%), were recorded as bearing some form of this index mark. If, however, the Carausian part of the hoard is considered, only twenty four coins out of one hundred recorded bear any form of *C* mark, but more significantly if the Carausian part of the hoard is normalised on the number of *L* mint coins then the *C* content is 0.47, and as such not significantly high. A better insight into the somewhat unusual nature of this hoard may be gained, not by seeing it as a hoard containing an unusually high fraction of *C* coins, which is a distorted view, but more as a hoard containing an unusually low fraction of unmarked types of Carausius.

It seems most unusual that a hoard also containing coins of the Gallic Empire should contain only four unmarked coins. This must bring into question the structure of the hoard, and whether or not Baldwin was shown the whole hoard or just a selection of the better specimens from it. The find is alleged to have been made in the rebuilding of an old wall, a few miles from Colchester, but other details are vague. The structure of the hoard and even its provenance must thus be treated with extreme suspicion.

The find coins from both recent excavations (Reece *ibid*) and those housed in Colchester museum which meet the criteria for inclusion in the survey, show a much lower ratio of *C* coins than would be expected at a site actually producing the latter, (0.37), this being close to the average ratio taking Britain as a whole. Thus, statistical evidence for the mint having been sited at Colchester is very weak, and archaeological evidence, does little to support any claim, (Hull *ibid* and Crummy 1987).

The purpose of a mint is to provide a good supply of money to the population and military personnel in its area. Geographically, Colchester, situated in a position sheltered from the bulk of the population by London, would seem, on a strategic basis, to be a poor location for a major mint. One may argue the parallel of Rome and Ostia, both having mints in the early fourth century, though in similar proximity, but that case was very different. Ostia was a major port concerned with the large scale importation of supplies for Italy, and as such would logistically be well situated as an extra mint; it is extremely unlikely that Colchester, as part of the 'independent' province of Britain, would have enjoyed a similar status. On the face of the evidence available it seems less than likely that Colchester housed the *C* mint.

The claims of *Clausentum* rest on two premises. Firstly, the abbreviation *CL* would fit the name much better, comprising of the first two letters of the name, and secondly, the logistical argument could be put forward that activity on the South Coast would necessitate the setting up of a fleet base, and that Southampton Water would be an ideal place for such. Eighteen coins of Carausius and five of Allectus were recorded as having turned up on the site (Mattingly 1932), but these should be placed in context. The number of coins of the Gallic Empire was large, making the British : Gallic ratio low. This certainly fails to indicate the increased activity expected in the establishment of such a headquarters.

Claims on behalf of *Clausentum* have been somewhat muted by archaeological evidence (Cotton and Gathercole 1958). The excavations, whilst unearthing a single coin of Allectus, admittedly of the *C* issue, and not a single coin of Carausius, found little evidence to suggest that the importance of late third century *Clausentum* was sufficient to merit the status of possession of a mint. There is no reason to suppose that the evidence of metal working unearthed had any direct link with the production of a coinage. Thus, on the basis

SITE	L	C	SP/SC	Unmk'd	RSR	Rouen
CIRENCESTER	64	20	11	96	1	2
PIERCEBRIDGE	34	11	12	52	1	1
RICHBOROUGH	82	30	39	179	2	4
COLCHESTER	66	25	10	101	1	2
SILCHESTER	68	29	25	115	-	1
CATTERICK	16	7	1	18	-	-
KENCHESTER	24	11	7	61	-	-
ALDBOROUGH	16	8	6	16	1	-
VERULAMIUM	58	30	11	99	1	-
LINCOLN	19	10	6	31	-	-
LYDNEY	12	14	3	21	1	-
TOTAL	459	175	131	799	8	10
	29.0%	11.1%	8.3%	50.5%	0.5%	0.6%

FIGURE 14 TABLE OF CARAUSIAN FINDS FROM MAJOR SITES (NUMBER OF COINS FOUND)
The TOTAL number of coins in this survey is 1582.
The totals were all arrived at by personal inspection of the coins, using the criteria outlined in the text, with the exception of the totals for Catterick, kindly provided by Mr P.J. Casey, and some coins from recent excavations at Cirencester, details of which were kindly supplied by Dr C.E. King.

SITE	L	C	SP/SC	Unmk'd
CIRENCESTER	1	0.31	0.17	1.50
PIERCEBRIDGE	1	0.32	0.35	1.52
RICHBOROUGH	1	0.36	0.47	2.18
COLCHESTER	1	0.37	0.15	1.53
SILCHESTER	1	0.42	0.37	1.69
CATTERICK	1	0.43	0.07	1.13
KENCHESTER	1	0.46	0.29	2.54
ALDBOROUGH	1	0.50	0.38	1.63
VERULAMIUM	1	0.52	0.19	1.71
LINCOLN	1	0.52	0.32	1.63
LYDNEY	1	1.16	0.25	1.75
ALL COINS	1	0.38	0.29	1.74

FIGURE 15 TABLE SHOWN IN FIGURE 14 NORMALISED ON L MARKED COINS
The TOTAL number of coins in this survey is 1582.
The totals were all arrived at by personal inspection of the coins, using the criteria outlined in the text, with the exception of the totals for Catterick, kindly provided by Mr P.J. Casey, and some coins from recent excavations at Cirencester, details of which were kindly supplied by Dr C.E. King.

of our evidence to date, *Clausentum* seems an unlikely contender for the *C* mint.

St. Davids, with its total absence of recorded Roman activity can be disregarded as a figment of Stukeley's over fertile imagination, whilst Catterick, with a relatively small yield of Carausian material has little in its favour.

In some respects *Calleva* has a reasonably strong claim. The British: Gallic ratio is high, at 0.48, echoing the high activity in the town under the British Empire. The amount of Carausian and Allectan coinage is prolific enough to suggest that it may well have had sufficient importance to possess a mint. The ratio of *C:L* coins (0.42) is, however, average and this fails to lend much weight to the argument in favour.

Another argument against *Calleva* being the site of a mint, is that also applied to *Camulodunum*, namely that its proximity to London makes it logistically unsound.

Glevum can be regarded as more of a suggestion based on a town fitting the index mark *GL*, than on archeological evidence, and by the late third century *Corinium* would have been a more economically thriving centre. We should not, however, discount the possibility put forward in an earlier chapter that an important fleet base, as yet undiscovered, may have been sited in either Lydney or possibly at *Glevum* itself. The high ratio of *C* coins found at Lydney would tie in with such a theory, but this is somewhat negated by only average numbers of such coins found at Kenchester, only thirty or so miles away.

Corinium shows signs of a high level of activity under Carausius. The ratio of British:Gallic coins, at 0.51 is one of the highest recorded and indicates that its importance could well have been in keeping with the siting of the second mint. This idea is somewhat destroyed by the very low ratio of *C:L* coins found at *Corinium, (0.31)*. This is the lowest of the sites recorded, and is even more surprising when considered against Lydney (1.16), Silchester (0.42) and Kenchester (0.46), all of which lie within 50 miles as the crow flies.

The evidence is thus extremely negative for any of these sites being the location for the *C* mint, and other possibilities should be explored. Place-names in Roman Britain that qualify for the *CL* abbreviation are limited (Rivet and Smith 1979). Only *Calcaria* (Tadcaster) fits in reasonably well, but any other evidence in its support is not forthcoming. Such an argument may be at least equally as well applied to Lincoln, with its status as a *Colonia*. The coin evidence from Lincoln, where the *C:L* ratio is 0.52, the highest of all the sites considered, except Lydney, is certainly more encouraging than that at Colchester (0.37) although the actual number of coins recorded from Lincoln is too small to be treated with conviction. Geographically, at least, Lincoln is situated in a more favourable position than many of the sites suggested.

It has been proposed, in their consideration of the case for Colchester, that *CL* might stand for *Colonia* rather than *Camulodunum* (Davies and Crummy 1987). If this were to be so, there is no reason to suppose that the *Colonia* at Lincoln would be a less worthy candidate for ownership of a mint than Colchester.

There is no evidence to suggest that the *C* coins were struck at Boulogne or anywhere else on the continent. They were struck throughout the reigns of both Carausius and Allectus, and it is likely that for much of this time the British Empire had no foothold, whatsoever, on the mainland of Europe.

The suggestion that the unmarked coins were struck in Boulogne (Carson 1971), can, in the light of all the evidence now available, retain little credence. This was based on the relative abundance of the unmarked coinage recovered from Richborough, where the ratio (2.18) is admittedly high. Carson then compared his figures with those from other sites, further from Boulogne which yielded significantly less unmarked coinage, and thus suggested that Boulogne could be the site of the unmarked mint. There are two factors which give strong indications that this attribution is very doubtful. Firstly, Kenchester, prolific in Carausian coinage, and a long way from the south east coast of Britain exhibits an even higher ratio, (2.54) of the unmarked coinage, and secondly, if this were the case, then the unmarked coinage could be expected to form a reasonably large portion of the continental finds of Carausius. The continental finds of Carausius have been listed by Loriot (Loriot 1978), and show the following breakdown. Of the thirty nine described finds, twenty bear some form of the *L* mark, eight the *C* mark, only six are of the unmarked coinage, with four attributed to the Rouen mint and one bearing the *RSR* mark.

Though such a theory has its attractions to those who believe that Boulogne was held until almost the very end of the reign of Carausius, before being lost, it would appear particularly dangerous to use the fact that Allectus issued no unmarked coinage, as evidence for the unmarked issues emanating from Boulogne. As discussed in an earlier chapter, the difficulty of maintaining a continental foothold at Boulogne for several years would appear extreme, and the alternative interpretation of the panegyric, presented in an earlier chapter, could indicate that it was, in fact, Allectus who strove to create a bridgehead at Boulogne.

Although one may well expect to find a predominance of *C* coins geographically near the source of issue, it must be remembered that the coins in circulation at this time do appear to mix with almost incredible rapidity. Hoards almost invariably display a cross section of coins from the various operational mints. This mixing is nowhere more acutely illustrated than in the fourth century, a period when some up to twenty mints were operational at any one time, spread right across the Empire. Finds in

HUGH P.G.WILLIAMS

Britain are not restricted to coins from the London, Trier or Lyons mints, although these predominate, but come from all over the Roman World. Fourth century finds from Canterbury illustrate this well, yielding a high proportion of coins from the mints mentioned above, but also coins struck at Arles, Rome, Aquileia, Siscia, Thessalonica, Constantinople and Cyzicus (Fulford 1978). If such mixing can take place so rapidly over such a large geographical area, then we must be aware that the *L, C* and unmarked coins, circulating in the confines of *Britannia*, would thus be expected to become well-mixed in a correspondingly short time, creating differences in ratio that are difficult to detect.

Nevertheless, in the absence of a geographical solution, other more unorthodox possibilities merit consideration. The possibilty that *C* may represent *Classiensis* and as such indicate the existence of a separate 'fleet' coinage (Bailey 1981), promotes an idea well out of keeping with mint practice in the Central Empire in the second half of the third century, where letters can normally be ascribed to cities housing the mint. *Britannia* under Carausius was, however, an entirely different situation. The idea of a 'fleet' coinage would not have been a totally new concept, since it could be argued that certain issues of Marc Antony may be regarded in this way. The fleet would have constituted an important part of the manpower resources available to Carausius, and tradition apart, there is no other reason to regard the suggestion as an impossibility. Numerical site evidence does, however, go some way towards destroying this theory.

Lydney, if we are to suppose a proximity to a naval base, yields coins overwhelmingly in favour of the theory, but here the encouragement ends. The six sites with the next highest proportions of *C* mint coins are Lincoln, St.Albans, Aldborough, Kenchester, Catterick and Silchester all far from the coast. The idea, therefore, that these coins were used in the payment of naval personnel must be treated with extreme doubt.

With the exception of the finds from Lydney, which was possibly a special case, the constitution of the coinage recovered from the other sites surveyed shows more uniformity than differences, and this must lead to consideration of the possibility that all the coins emanated from one central location, namely London. There are enough stylistic differences between the coins to suggest that they come from separate establishments, though there is no reason why these should not be different workshops or *officinae* housed under the same roof. There are also policy differences that manifest themselves later in the reign. The famous three-headed types of Carausius and his Brother Emperors (Plate 2 No.5) are issued at the *C* mint only, as is the unorthodox,

but striking, full-faced portrait representation of the Emperor (Plate 2 No.13).

Such a tri-partite mint would create the possibility for the coinage to be issued in a mixed form for distribution, opening the possibility that each establishment struck, on behalf of different 'sponsors' for a central distribution pool. Each destination would then receive a coinage mixed at source.

Alternatively, the coins produced at each establishment could have been destined for circulation via the payment of three or more social groups. In this idea, Bailey may have not been too far wrong. It is clear, from the distribution of finds, that the concept of a fleet coinage is doubtful, but the rider that *L* may indicate *Legionensis*, and as such represent that part of the exchequer involved in army pay remains plausible. As such, military pay, would probably pass quickly into circulation and spread uniformly throughout the province. A possibility that would ensure a similar spread and rapid circulation for the *C* coinage would be that it could represent the payment of the 'civil service' administration that undoubtedly existed on various levels throughout the province. The relative abundance of the two coinages would tally with the concept that more military personnel were on the paylist than civil administrators. The unmarked coinage could then possibly represent the general circulation coinage needs of the civilian population.

Acceptance of such a system would also present the added attraction of locating the extra-ordinary issues such as *RSR* , which may well stand for *Rationalis Summae Rei*, or Chief Finance Ministry, and the as yet unexplained *BRI* mark in the same premises.

Such a solution is, of course very conjectural, and is not in keeping with the orthodox mint practice of the Central Empire, but it would go some way to producing a workable theory that would tie in with the distribution, relative abundance and differing stylistic trends exhibited by the coinage.

The distribution of the small issue of coins of a most distinctive style usually referred to as the 'Rouen' type is also worthy of some consideration. The early dating of these coins has been discussed in a preceding chapter. These issues do, however, turn up on British sites, and their spread through the province was plotted initially by Loriot (Loriot 1978). Since this original article was published, several more such coins of known provenance has come to light. A modified map illustrates their spread through a wide circulation area encompassing much of Southern Britain (figure 16).

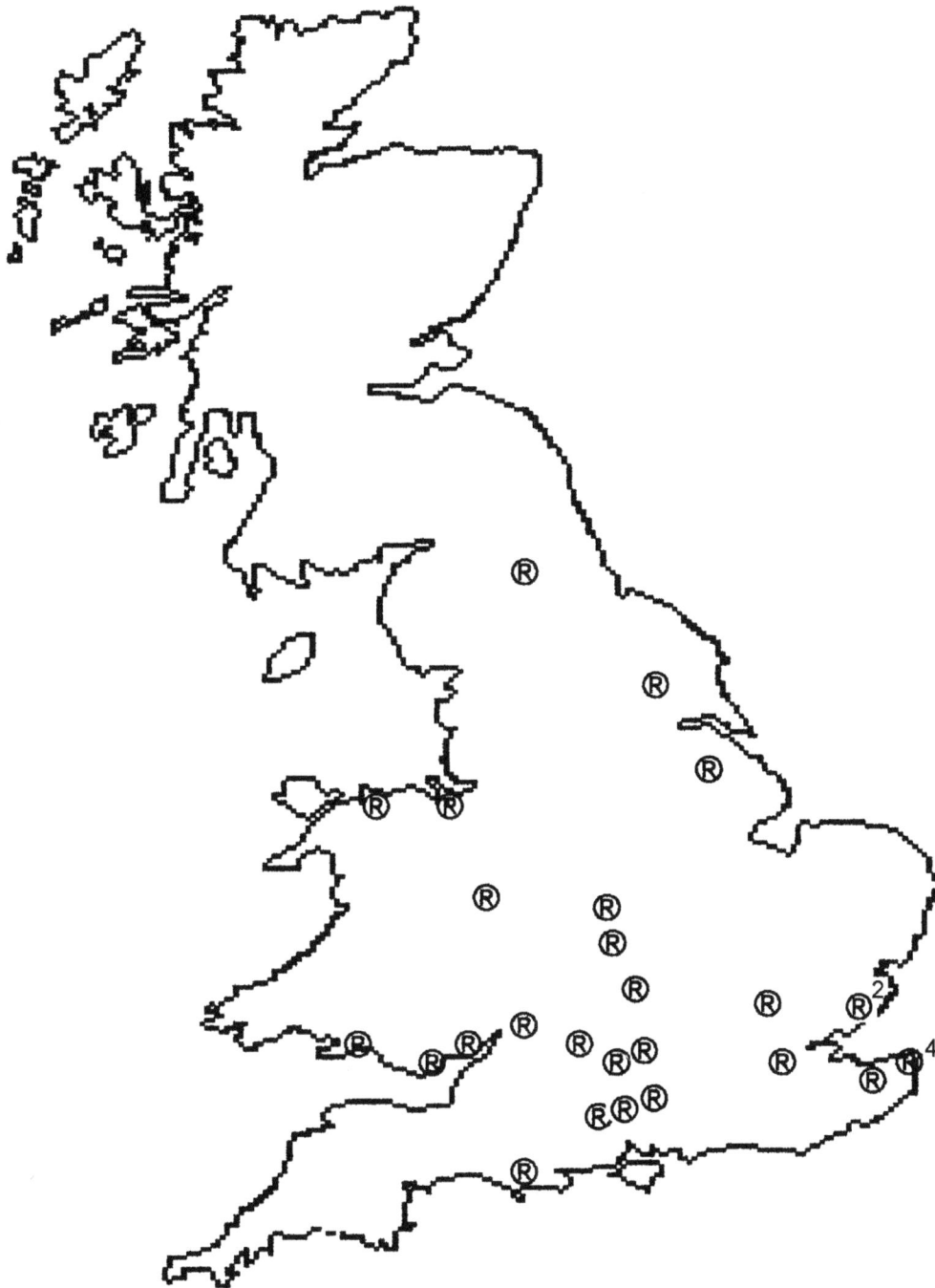

FIGURE 16 MAP OF ROUEN STYLE COIN FINDS
This map updates the one produced by Loriot (Loriot 1978). Finds recorded since the original article show a wide circulation area encompassing the southern half of Britain.

Chapter Eight

Carausian Coin Hoards

A comprehensive listing of Carausian coin hoards was published by Shiel (Shiel 1977). This lists many hoards discovered in the eighteenth and nineteenth centuries, which have long since been dispersed. The constitutional details of such hoards must, in many cases, be regarded with a certain amount of suspicion. The completeness of this listing also necessitates that hoards, or accumulations registered sometimes include only a single Carausian coin. Such accumulations must be treated with reserve, since careless excavation may sometimes introduce stray coins to the group. These caveats need to be stated, but it should be remembered that the list also includes some major well-recorded hoards on which much of the earlier work on the coinage of Carausius is based.

Since this work several important new hoards, notably those from Normanby (Bland and Burnett 1988), Dorchester (King forthcoming), Baylham (Williams forthcoming) and Lacock (Bland 1992), have come to light, whilst a much older hoard from Croydon has been successfully reconstituted by Burnett (Burnett 1984). A further hoard that was found about 1987, and taken to Germany to be dispersed in trade before any expert examination was possible represents a sad loss to the progress of numismatic knowledge of the period.

Before drawing any conclusions from hoard-evidence , the more important earlier hoards should be summarised, alongside details from the recent discoveries. The hoards may be divided into four main groups.

Group A
Hoards which terminate with Carausian coins from the first part of the reign. (These hoards terminate with coins of the index mark F/O/ML or earlier, on the chronology outlined in a previous chapter, and were probably deposited between late 286 and early 290). The group may be further sub-divided into those hoards with a small Carausian content ratio (Group A1) and those with a large one, (Group A2). An initial listing is given below, with the percentage of Carausian coins :-

GROUP A1		GROUP A2	
Bredicot, Worc.	(3%)	Baylham, Suffolk	(96%)
Dorchester, Dorst.	(0.7%)	Canterbury, Kent	(93%)
Normanby, Lincs.	(0.15%)	Croydon, Surrey	(92%)
Penard, S. Glam.	(3.1%)	Din Silwy, A'sey	(72%)
Wentwood, Gwent	(1%)	Linchmere,Sus'x	(66%)
		L.Orme I, Caer	(97%)
		L.Orme II, Caer	(89%)
		Margaretting, E'x	(63%)
		S.Norwood, Kent	(87%)
		Verulamium,Hts	(100%)

Group B
Hoards which terminate with coins of Carausius struck in the latter part of the reign. As for the hoards in Group A, a similar subdivision can take place. Those with a small Carausian content ratio being Group B1.

GROUP B1		GROUP B2	
Erw Hên, Dyfed	(1%)	Gt.Orme, Caern	(76%)
Hoveringham, Notts	(14%)	Silchester, Hants	(82%)
Llangeinwen, A'sey	(30%)	Bicester	(100%)
		1987 Hoard	

The 1987 Hoard is included here. It is discussed in detail later, though the non-Carausian element in the hoard is as yet unsubstantiated.

Group C
 These are hoards which terminate under Allectus. Again this group may be subdivided into those containing a large ratio of earlier coinage, and those possessing a high ratio of British Empire coins.

GROUP C1		GROUP C2	
Blackmoor, Hants (2.6%)		Colchester, Essex	(91%)
Crondall, Hants *		Burton Latimer, N'hnts (99%)	
Holt, Norfolk,	(1%)		
Lilly Horn, Glos.	(1%)		
Oundle, Northants *			
Skewen, Glam. *			
	Watchfield, Berks (52%)		

* = Information about constitution of hoard not complete, but a low Carausian/Allectan content is definite.

Group D
Group D forms an intriguing, and certainly problematical group of hoards, often referred to as Legitimist Hoards. The constitution of these hoards is largely consistent of coins of the Central Empire, with little representation from the Gallic usurpers or Carausius and Allectus. The coins have obviously been well-sorted, but the hoards contain coins issued by Carausius in the names of Diocletian and Maximian.

GROUP D
Cadbury, Somerset
Cheddar, Somerset
East Harnham, Wilts
Evenley, Northants
Gloucester (Cross), Glos.
 Lacock, Wilts
Rogiet, Monmouthshire
Langtoft, East Yorkshire

Nc = Number of coins of Carausius   Na= Number of coins of Allectus
Nt = Total number of coins in hoard
* = approximate number   U = information not available

Find Location	Type	Nc	Na	Nt
Bredicot, Worc	A1	4	0	62
Dorchester, Dorset	A1	72	0	10,000*
Normanby, Lincs	A1	73	0	47,912
Penard, S.Glamorgan	A1	81	0	2,583
Wentwood, Monmouthshire	A1	12	0	1,051
Erw Hen, Carmarthenshire	B1	9	0	684
Hoveringham, Notts	B1	40	0	289
Llangeinwen, Anglesey	B1	7	0	23
'1987' Hoard	B1-B2	200+	0	U
Blackmoor, Hants	C1	522	78	22,436
Crondall, Hants	C1	25*	7*	200+
Holt, Norfolk	C1	9	2	1,012
Lilly Horn, Glos	C1	7	1	1,223
Oundle, Northants	C1	7	1+	1,203
Skewen, S.Glamorgan	C1	18+	1+	61+
Baylham, Suffolk	A2	54	0	56
Canterbury, Kent	A2	107	0	109
Croydon, Surrey	A2	81+	0	88+
Din Silwy, Anglesey	A2	44	0	61
Linchmere, Sussex	A2	534	0	810
Little Orme 1, Caern	A2	556+	0	576+
Little Orme 2, Caern	A2	51	0	67
Margaretting, Essex	A2	20	0	32
Verulamium, Herts	A2	19	0	19
South Norwood, Kent	A2	48	0	55
Great Orme, Caern	B2	13	0	17
Silchester, Hants	B2	18	0	22
Colchester, Essex	C2	102	167	298
Burton Latimer, Northants	C2	58(+1)	48	108
Watchfield, Berks	C2-C1	6	6	23
Cadbury, Somerset	D	1(+2)	0	37
Cheddar, Somerset	D	0(+7)	0	99
East Harnham, Wilts	D	0(+46)	0	3,938
Gloucester, Glos	D	20(+16)	2	15,546
Lacock, Wilts	D	1(+8)	1	93
Rogiet, Monmouthshie	D	17(+7)	3+748Q+11i	3,778
Langtoft A, East Yorks	D	1(+U)	1(+U)	578+398

Numbers in brackets indicate coins in name of Diocletian/Maximian issued by Carausius
Q = small galley Q radiates   i = irregular

FIGURE 17 TABLE OF CONTENTS OF MAJOR CARAUSIAN HOARDS

Shiel (Shiel ibid) deals with coin hoards containing Carausian material that terminate at dates after the eventual overthrow of Allectus. Such an exercise will yield little information as to the picture of coinage under the British Empire. Most such hoards are Constantinian, though some are a little later. Admittedly some Constantinian hoards contain one or two Carausian pieces, but in reality they probably represent exceptions that probably remained in circulation for a few years in error. A few of the hoards quoted by Shiel are accumulations of coins reaching across two centuries or more. These are more likely to represent lost collections of Romano-British, Saxon, or Mediaeval numismatists, pieced together from field finds and then subsequently lost again. Those major hoards listed above need to be re-examined in the context of what information they may yield.

Group A1
Our knowledge of this type of hoard has been greatly improved by the discovery of two large hoards at Normanby in Lincolnshire (47,912 coins) and at Dorchester in Dorset (approximately 10,000 coins). These two hoards bear great similarity to one another in their contents. Both end with a very small representation of coins of Carausius and were, in all probability, buried during the very first few months of the reign. Similar in many ways, though of a much smaller scale are those hoards from Penard, South Glamorgan, and Wentwood in Gwent. The hoard from Bredicot in Worcestershire, though records are incomplete, probably also belongs to this group. A more detailed analysis of each hoard is given below.

Bredicot, Worcestershire: first mentioned by J.Allies in his History of Worcestershire. 1852.

Records of this find are sketchy. A red earthenware pot containing 140 'third brass' was found in 1839, during the construction of the Gloucester-Birmingham railway. Details are only recorded of 62 of the coins, which contained a sizeable majority of Gallic empire coins and terminated with four coins of Carausius. No further details survive.

Dorchester, Dorset   Details of this hoard, and the chance to examine the Carausian element, was kindly provided by Dr. C.E. King of the Ashmolean Museum, where it is currently awaiting detailed examination and publication.

The hoard contains an estimated 10,000 coins and terminates with a mere 72 of Carausius. This fact, coupled with the index marks on the coins, indicates a concealment date of very early in the reign.

35 of the coins are definitely unmarked, with another 28, on which the exergue is either incomplete or illegible, probably so.

There is only one coin, with the early ML mark from the L mint, and no representative at all from the C mint. Also present are four coins with unorthodox index marks, a thunderbolt, V/ /* ; V/*/ ; and XX. The style of the busts on the coins bearing V as the index mark links them firmly with the unmarked series. One coin yields the unusual legend IMPCARAVSIVSPFIAVG, giving evidence that the Emperor used the Invictus title early in the reign.

There is, unusually for the reign, evidence of shared dies and even one die link between two different obverse dies and a Laetitia reverse type.

The style of the busts used on half the obverse dies is so stylistically linked as to assume that these dies emanated from the same workshop, or even the same hand.

The presence in the hoard of one RSR coin and three from the Rouen mint give important backing to the theory that both these issues took place at the beginning of the reign.

Another interesting observation is that eleven of the Carausian coins show clear details of being overstruck on earlier coins, and as many as twenty show some sign of being so. This again illustrates that when the need for coinage, and its propaganda value, was acute, that coins already in circulation formed ready made blanks.

Normanby, Lincolnshire   This hoard was found in 1985, about one and a half miles north of the Roman settlement at Owmby. (Bland and Burnett 1988). The hoard contained 47,912 coins, predominantly of Gallienus or the Gallic Emperors, which terminated with a mere handful of seventy three of Carausius, including four which were deemed to be irregular.

There is minimal representation of Central Empire coinage from the time of Aurelian, 270-5, to that of Diocletian. In this respect the content of the Hoard mirrors that of the previously discussed hoard from Dorchester, and that from Erw Hˆn in Dyfed, (Boon 1966). The small Carausian element, and the style and index marks on the coins give a likely concealment date of early in the reign, probably in the immediate months after Carausius secured Britain.

A breakdown of the Carausian content of the hoard is as follows:-

Unmarked Issues	54
'Rouen'	1
R.S.R.	3
'L' Issues	5
'C' Issues	6
Irregular	4

There is little reason to suppose that the hoard is anything other than from early in the reign, thus giving further evidence for the early issue of both the 'Rouen' and R.S.R. coinages. The hoard also yields a further provenance for a 'Rouen' coin, indicating the speed with which their circulation area increased during the first few months of the regime.

The coins from the 'L' mint bear the early marks, ML; L/ /ML and F/O/ML, whilst those from the 'C' Mint bear the contemporary marks of C; MC and the relatively rare combination of F/O/C.

Bland and Burnett argue that the existence of a coin, though not from the hoard, citing a fourth Tribunic power possessing a 'C' index mark, indicates a much later date for these issues, and thus a later burial date for this hoard.. The whole issue of the dated coins of Carausius is looked at in a later chapter, and the early deposition of this hoard is postulated.

Penard, Glamorgan   This hoard was discovered in 1966 at Penard on the Gower Peninsula. The hoard was seized by the Gowerton Police on behalf of the coroner, and although 2,583 coins were recovered , the original total may have been higher, (Boon 1967) . As with both Normanby and Dorchester the majority of the coins are of Gallienus, Claudius and the Gallic Emperors. The hoard terminates with eighty one coins of Carausius, alongside four issues of Diocletian, all dated to 286, and one of Maximian, tentatively dated to 290 - 294. The hoard contains three RSR. issues and also a single 'Rouen' piece. The majority of the coins are, however, unmarked, though one has an obverse bust very reminiscent of that found on the rare BRI issues; a 'BRI' coin has since been found nearby at Minchin Hole (Boon 1994).

The index marks seem to end with the F/O/ML issue, with two notable exceptions. Firstly, there is the coin of Maximian which is dated by R.I.C. to 290-4, and secondly there are two later Carausian issues that are alleged to be from the hoard. The former of these is a fragment of a B/E/ MLXXI issue and the latter a VIRTVS AVGGG type with the mark S/P/C.

Without these issues a concealment date not long after that of the Normanby hoard could be speculated upon, but these issues cause some uncertainty. Whilst it is possible that they represent burial of the hoard sometime from 291 onwards, caution must be exercised and two other possibilities remain.

Firstly, it is possible that the coins may have been later additions to the hoard, whilst secondly they may have been interlopers introduced to the hoard during its undoubtedly inexpert excavation.

Wentwood, Gwent   This hoard was discovered in 1860 and the original records suggest that it contained between 1200 and 1300 coins, (Lee 1862). At present the National Museum of Wales holds just over 1000 of the coins. The

majority of the coins are of Gallienus, Claudius and the Gallic Emperors, and the hoard terminates with twelve coins of Carausius. These are mostly of the unmarked type, and the hoard concludes with a specimen marked F/O/ML. In content this hoard fits in well with the others in this group.

Group A2
This forms the largest group of major hoard finds. The Carausian element of the hoards in Group A1 comprises no more than 4% of the total number of coins in any of those hoards. Group A2, whilst seemingly consisting of hoards also concealed near the beginning of the regime, comprises a large group of hoards in which the Carausian content is always above 60% of the total, and in most cases is over 85%.

Whereas most of these hoards have been known for many years, they are, in some cases, overdue for re-appraisal. A recently discovered hoard from Baylham in Suffolk is an important addition to the group, as is a yet unpublished hoard from Canterbury and second hoard Little Ormes Head, also awaiting publication. Andrew Burnett, (Burnett and Casey 1984), has performed an excellent task in reconstituting the Croydon Hoard of 1893, whilst a new look at a hoard discovered during the Wheeler excavations at Verulamium, (Wheeler and Wheeler 1936), yields an interesting insight into the coinage of the Period. A summary of some of the important issues raised by each hoard is outlined below.

Baylham, Suffolk   This hoard was discovered in late 1988 as a result of a chance metal-detector find of two coins of Carausius, fused together by corrosion. This subsequently led to the discovery of fifty four further coins of Carausius, and two of earlier date (Williams forthcoming). The coins had been scattered by earlier ploughing and were all found in an area approximately 6 metres by 2 metres, which the finder, Mr. James Woodrow excavated to a depth of about three-quarters of a metre. My sincere thanks must go to the finder for allowing me access to examine the finds, and also to Jude Plouviez of the Suffolk Archaeological Unit for informing me of the find.It is quite possible that the two earlier coins, an extremely worn as of Severus Alexander, and an antoninianus of Claudius II from the Rome mint, (R.I.C.45), are both strays from the same area, but it seems more than likely that all fifty four Carausian coins emanate from the same hoard, these having been scattered by successive ploughings of the area. No trace of a container was found.

The style of the coins, together with a study of their exergual marks, suggest a deposition date of early in the reign. Seven of the coins, and possibly an eighth (a legionary issue) bear index marks of the L mint, the latest being a single L/ /ML issue, whilst only one, the only other legionary type in the hoard, bears the index mark MSC. One coin bears the enigmatic mark XXI.

The remaining coins, forty four in total, all appear to be unmarked, though in the case of those few coins where the exergue is off the flan, this attribution is conjectural and is based on style. As is invariably the case with early Carausian material the judgement between official coin and unofficial copy is based on a hazy and subjective border line. Of the fifty four coins in question though, only seven might be regarded as possibly being unofficial.

Interestingly the hoard contained no Rouen or RSR. coins, and significantly the C mint contributed only a single coin. If the suggestion of the location of the C mint being at Colchester is to be considered, then surely its proximity to Baylham (20 miles) would be expected to generate a greater representation of 'C' marked coins.

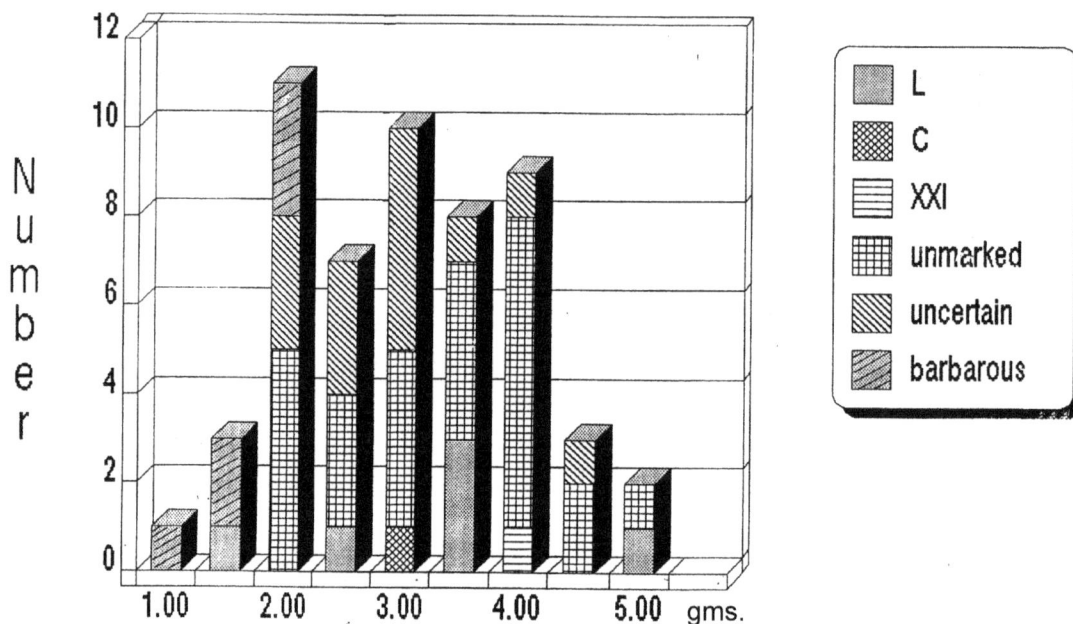

FIGURE 18 METROLOGY OF THE BAYLHAM HOARD

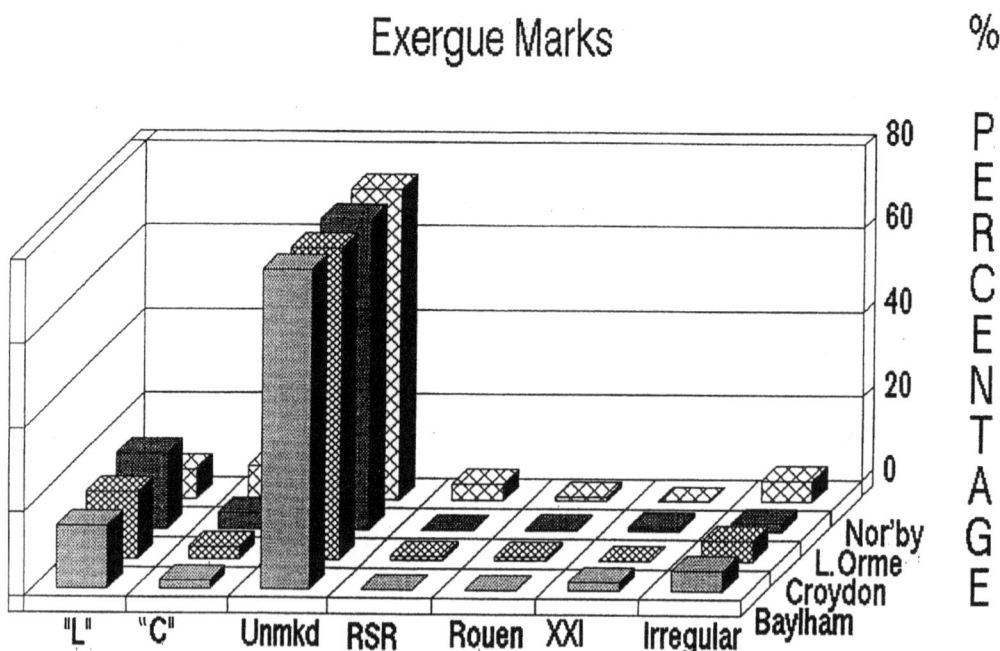

FIGURE 19 COMPARISON OF BAYLHAM HOARD WITH OTHERS

The following pages illustrate the metrology of the Carausian element of the Baylham Hoard, and also illustrate a direct comparison with other early Carausian hoards, namely Little Orme I, Croydon and Normanby (figures 17 and 18).

Canterbury, Kent   This hoard was examined by Shiel (Shiel 1977), who reports that it contained 117 coins, of which 109 were of Carausius. The latest index mark present was F/O/ML , indicating a deposition early in the reign.

Croydon, Surrey   This hoard, originally discovered in 1893, was reassembled after two groups of coins with Croydon provenance were found in the trays of London dealers in 1970.

As is typical of this group, a large number of the pieces, at least fifty seven out of the eighty eight re-assembled, were unmarked, and as with the Canterbury hoard , the coins terminate with the F/O/ML mark. The hoard contains one Rouen coin and another with the RSR index mark, further confirmation of the early issue date of both types.

Din Silwy (or Bwrydd Arthur), Anglesey   This hoard, housed in the National Museum of Wales consists of sixty one antoniniani, terminating with the index mark F/O/ML , most of the forty four Carausian coins appear to be unmarked, though several specimens have a thick coating of varnish on the reverse making identification difficult.

Linchmere, Sussex   This hoard was discovered in 1924, close to the point where the counties of Surrey, Sussex and Hampshire meet, (Webb 1925). The hoard contained eight hundred and twelve coins including five hundred and thirty-four of Carausius. These terminate with three hundred and seventy-four all bearing the mark F/O/ML and one with the mark MCXXI, giving a possible concealment date of early 290. The information outlined above fails to give indication of several unorthodox features of the hoard.

The most striking first impression of an examination of this hoard is the excellent condition of the coins, allied to the fact that they are almost invariably on large well rounded flans, almost as if the hoarder had chosen them for their technical excellence. The non-Carausian element of the hoard is not, as is usually the case, predominated by coins of the Gallic Emperors, but contains 275 coins of the Central Empire, from Aurelian to Maximian, and only three specimens of the Western usurpers.

Although all indications suggest that the unmarked coinage of Carausius was the most abundant in the early years of the reign, only thirty three of the coins of Carausius are unmarked. Four hundred and sixty-four of the coins bear L marks and only thirty-seven carry marks attributed to the C mint. The large number of F/O/ML

coins could be construed to indicate that a consignment of coinage, so marked, had arrived directly from the mint to the owner of the hoard. The presence of the large element of Central Empire coinage makes this less likely, and it would seem that the owner put together a cache of well struck and stylistically pleasing coins with some deliberation. This would explain the apparent lack of early unmarked coins, the majority of which are hurriedly struck on small and often re-used blanks.

Little Orme's Head I, Caernarvonshire This major hoard consisted of at least seven hundred coins, of which four hundred and twenty-four were collected by Dr. Willoughby Gardner (Gardner 1908), who also gathered details of two hundred and forty-three further coins, the list being eventually published by H.A.Seaby (Seaby 1956). Many of the coins from this hoard have now been acquired by the major museums such as the British Museum, the National Museum of Wales, the Ashmolean Museum, the Fitzwilliam Museum and Manchester Museum. All but thirteen of the coins were issued by Carausius, and the marked issues terminate with the F/O/ML and MCXXI issues. Rouen and RSR are represented by three and one coin respectively.

The index marks suggest a burial date close to that of the Linchmere hoard, though the overall content is stylistically very different. Well over four hundred of the coins are unmarked, and though they show a great variety of style, and in some cases artistic excellence, they are for the most part on small flans, of the type avoided, in all probability, by the Linchmere hoarder.

One of the unmarked antoniniani (Plate 7 Nos.14-15), now in the British Museum, bears a well-executed armed bust which shares an obverse die with the RSR aureus (Plate 2 No.6) in the BibliothŠque Nationale in Paris. This die-sharing between unmarked copper and R.S.R. gold could be construed as further evidence of the geographical proximity of the two production centres and opens up the possibility that they may even have been housed under the same roof.

Little Orme's Head II, Caernarvonshire   This second hoard was discovered at Little Orme's Head in the early 1980's. Though much smaller than the previous hoard, its content is, in many ways, similar to the former. The presence of three coins with the index mark S/P/C does, however, date its deposition a little later, maybe to the first half of 291. Examination of the hoard, now housed at the National Museum of Wales, showed a total of sixty seven coins, with fifty-one being of Carausius, ten were completely illegible, with three of Tetricus I, two of Victorinus and one of Claudius II. Twenty nine of the Carausian coins were unmarked, with a further nine probably so, though their exergues were either missing or unclear.

Margaretting, Essex This small hoard of 32 Antoniniani was discovered in 1930. Twenty of the coins are of

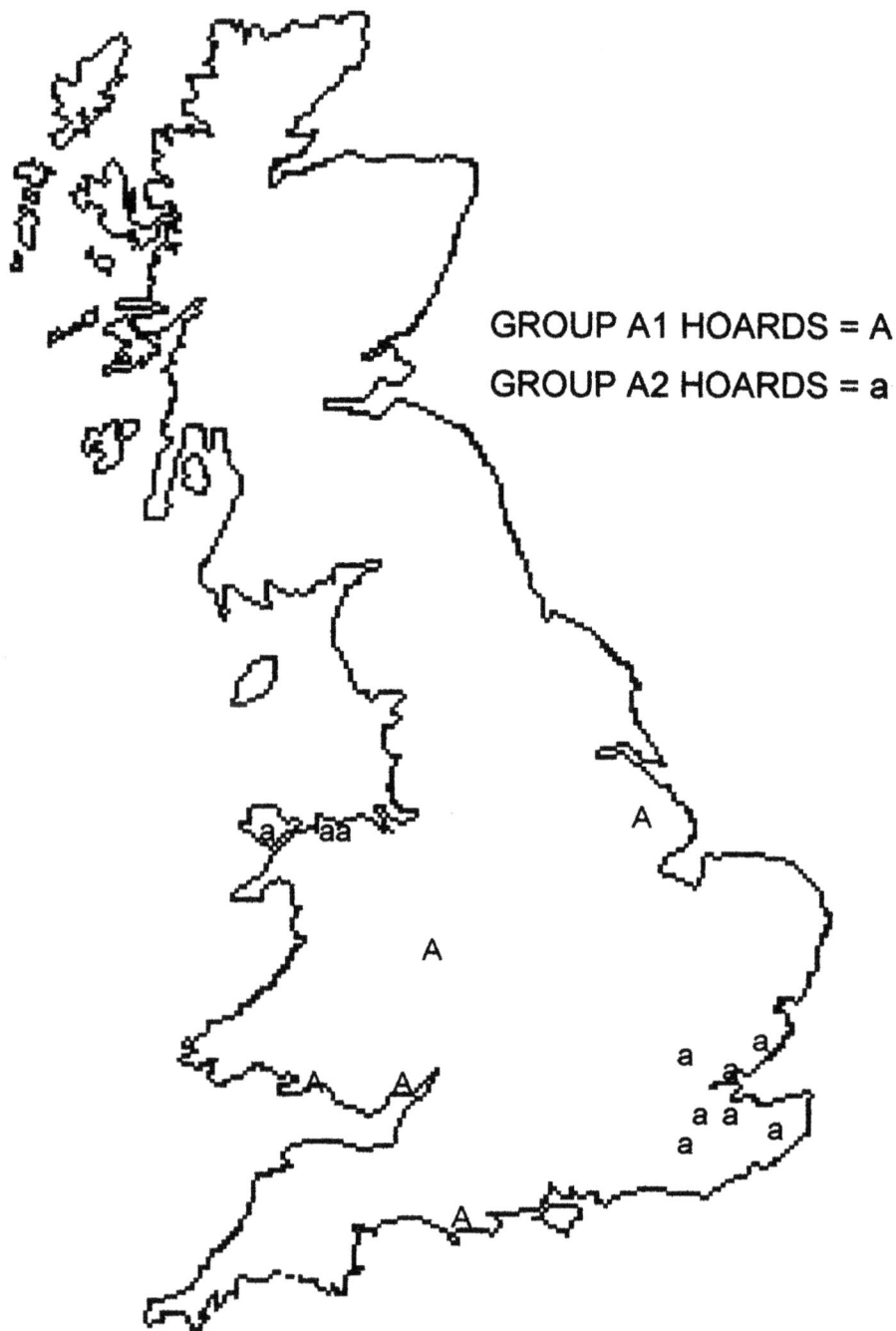

GROUP A1 HOARDS = A
GROUP A2 HOARDS = a

FIGURE 20 MAP OF GROUP A HOARDS

Carausius, the majority of which are unmarked (Colchester Museum Report, 1932).

South Norwood, Kent This hoard comprises of 55 antoniniani, of which 48 are of Carausius (Shiel 1977). Only four of the Carausian coins possess index marks, all being ML.

Verulamium, Herts This small hoard was discovered during excavations at Verulamium, and was originally published with sparse detail in the excavation report (Wheeler and Wheeler 1936). Examination of the coins, now in Verulamium Museum, gives much interesting information (Williams 1990). The hoard consists of nineteen coins, all of Carausius, fifteen are unmarked, one is marked IM (presumably for LM), and two are marked as ML. Though the hoard is small, its importance lies in the number of coins sharing identical dies. No fewer than ten of the coins were struck from the same pair of dies, and an eleventh, found in the same immediate area of the excavations, also possesses matching dies.

52

The reverse of these coins is unmarked, showing Pax with attributes of cornucopia, and a most distinctive olive branch, which is so exaggerated that it more resembles a Romano-British oak tree (Plate 6 Nos. 9-10). The final G in the legend is represented by a letter not unlike a modern S. The coin bearing the IM mark has a similar unorthodox final letter on its reverse, with a bust on the obverse of such similar style that it might be reasonable to suppose that it originated from the same workshop, or even the same engraver's hand. A further unmarked coin, though not die-linked, has an obverse bust of such similarity to those previously mentioned, that a case could be made that it, too, had the same origin.

The two coins bearing the ML mark also share common dies, and if regarded as official must be regarded as a product of the L mint. Even more important is the observation that the obverse die-links to that on one of the unmarked coins. Again, if all three coins are regarded as official issues, this is evidence of L and unmarked issues being struck alongside one another.

Coins sharing dies are not a common feature in Carausian hoards, and the constitution of this particular hoard makes it more than likely that the coins were buried close to their origin either geographically or in time. It is difficult to ascertain how much circulation the coins have seen, as they have all suffered badly from pitting due to fire damage.

Whether all, some, or any of the coins are official issues or contemporary copies, is, in the case of these typical early issues, a question whose answer depends on a certain element of subjective opinion. The coins appear to have been struck, rather than cast, with their flans bearing none of the similarities in shape that casting might be expected to yield. The style of the more sharply struck and less damaged coins is good, with obverse portraits comparable to those on much of the early coinage of the reign. The reverse types do, however, show certain elements of unorthodoxy in their representations of the figures' attributes. The mass of the coins is of a reasonable standard, especially when consideration is given to the possible effects of fire damage.

If the coins are regarded as contemporary copies then the probability of the forger being based at Verulamium is strong. If, on the other hand, the coins are official productions, then some interesting possibilities lie open for discussion. Had the coins been freshly brought from London to Verulamium just prior to loss or concealment? Did the L mint also issue unmarked coins or, even more conjectural, was a travelling workshop under the authority of the L mint, and using dies produced there, operational at Verulamium near the beginning of the reign?

Group B1
These hoards terminate late in the reign, and comprise of a small portion of Carausian coins in company with a predomination of antoniniani of Gallienus, Claudius II and the Gallic usurpers.

Erw Hˆn, Dyfed This hoard is now shared between the National Museum of Wales at Cardiff, and Carmarthen Museum. The find spot was two miles from the Roman gold mines at Dolaucothi (Boon 1966). The hoard, which was found in 1965, consisted of six hundred and eighty-two antoniniani of which only eight were Carausian issues. The latest being an issue bearing the index mark S/C/.

Boon cites the "meagre total and sub-standard character" of the small Carausian element as evidence that the neighbouring mines were not, at that time, under official direct government control. Such an assumption seems dangerous, especially when comparison is made with the Blackmoor Hoard (Bland 1982), where a large element of coinage from the Gallic Empire is found in company with many poor quality Carausian products in a hoard that in all probability constituted an "official" military pay-chest.

Hoveringham, Notts. This hoard, discovered in 1949, and published in the Numismatic Chronicle of that year, terminates with forty coins of Carausius, the latest index mark present being B/E/MLXXI.

Llangeinwen, Anglesey This is a small hoard (published in Arch.Cambrensis, 1856, p.326) of twenty-two or twenty-three coins, which was unearthed in the mid-nineteenth century. The single coin of Constantine I, is, in all probability a stray, and the hoard terminates with seven coins of Carausius, the latest being index-marked B/E/MLXXI.

Group B2
The content of this group of hoards terminates with Carausian issues from the second half of the reign, and yields a predominance of coins issued by that emperor. Two hoards are worthy of mention.

Great Orme's Head, Caernarvonshire This is a small hoard, located in the National Museum of Wales, consisting of seventeen coins, thirteen of which are Carausian. The final index-marks are B/E/MLXXI or S/C/C, these marks being, in all probability, contemporary with one another.

Silchester, Hants This is another small hoard, discovered in 1897, and now housed in Reading Museum . Eighteen of the twenty two coins in the hoard are Carausian, the latest bearing the index mark S/P/ML, indicating a burial date near the end of Carausius' reign, or just after the beginning of Allectus' term of power.

Bicester Hoard This small hoard consisted of seventeen coins of Carausius, one of which was issued in the name of Maximian. The latest coins in this hoard were the one mentioned above and two others bearing AVGGG in the reverse legend. (King 1982).

53

GROUP B1 HOARDS = B
GROUP B2 HOARDS = b

FIGURE 21 MAP OF GROUP B HOARDS

The 1987 Hoard   Lack of evidence of a find spot, and an approximate find date have resulted in this hoard of major importance being referred to throughout this work as the "1987 Hoard". Its overall constitution remains shrouded in mystery but it is almost certainly a Group B hoard.

The hoard is alleged to have been unearthed by a metal-detector user and taken to Germany for cleaning and dispersal in trade. The knowledge that may have been gained by thorough examination of this most important hoard cannot be over-emphasised, and the loss to numismatic research caused by its dispersal is incalculable.

The coins began appearing in auction sales and in dealers' trays from 1987 onwards. The coins have a most distinctive jet-black patina, and are in superb condition, struck on large flans.

Many enquiries have been made as to the discovery and

54

content of the hoard, and several rumours have circulated. The information listed below as to the nature of the hoard was pieced together from conversations with many people in the coin-trade, and after much sifting of the evidence seems to be the most reliable and complete version of events available at present.

The find spot seems, in all probability, to have been somewhere in the New Forest area of Hampshire. (rumours of Lincolnshire or even Boulogne seem unlikely). The finder left the country soon after the discovery was made. The hoard was concealed in a large pot filled to the brim. The hoard terminated with coins of Carausius, there being no Allectan element present. There were apparently no Carausian coins with the legend ending in AVGGG. One of the coins bore the rare index mark BRI. The suggestion has been put forward that there were many Gallic Empire coins in the hoard, this seems unlikely since no obvious emergence of such has been forthcoming.

The fact that many of the coins so far dispersed are of scarce or rare types, makes it likely that there are many more common types still to appear on the market. Details of coins that possess every probability of having come from this hoard have been noted throughout the period of this research project and an attempt is made at the end of this chapter to re-constitute part of this hoard, giving details of some one hundred and forty-four coins.

Group C1
This group of hoards terminates with coins of Allectus, but the hoards contain a vast majority of coins from earlier reigns, notably of the Gallic usurpers, Gallienus and Claudius II. They usually have minimal representation from the issues of the Central Empire from 273 to 296. The content of these hoards provides the best evidence of the constitution of the coinage in circulation during the reigns of the British Emperors. Thus, it seems likely that the earlier coinage of the Gallic usurpers and their contemporaries remained in circulation, forming an important part of the coinage. Any argument that these hoards were buried as demonetised and worthless coins, no longer passable under the Allectan regime must be invalidated by the inclusion of obviously current Allectan coins, though the possibility does exist that some may have been buried in such circumstances following the recapture of Britain by Constantius, and the coinage reform that followed (Eichholz 1953). This does not, however, affect the main observation that the earlier radiates were in circulation, alongside British issues throughout the period in question.

Blackmoor, Hampshire This is one of the largest and most important hoards from Roman Britain. It was discovered in 1873, and contained 29,802 coins, terminating with 635 coins of Carausius and Allectus, and one of Constantius, as counted by Lord Selbourne on whose land it was found and into whose possession it passed. Although the hoard had been examined by several eminent numismatists, including Webb, during the first half of the present century, the decision of the then present Lord Selbourne to auction the hoard at Christies in 1975 encouraged fresh analysis (Shiel 1975). As comprehensive a listing as was possible and detailed analysis of the hoard was published by Bland (Bland 1982). The size and nature of the hoard lead to the observation made by Bland that "it is hard to escape the conclusion that its burial must be connected with the advance of Constantius I's general from his landfall" towards his decisive final battle with the forces of Allectus. Lord Selbourne's original report cites the finding of a considerable number of swords and broken spears within a mile of the find spot, perhaps indicating that the battle took place in the immediate area of the find.

The Blackmoor Hoard contained many unusual types, and amongst the Carausian issues there were many of early style that posed questions as to whether or not they were regular issues. The question of regularity is discussed elsewhere in this thesis, but the observation by Bland after study of the Blackmoor coins is in agreement with Shiel (Shiel 1977) that in view of the very unorthodox die-axes, especially on the earlier issues, such a criterion is not a sound one for determining which coins are official and which irregular.

Holt, Norfolk This hoard, originally reported in 1944, (J.R.S. XXXIV, 1944), consisted of 1,105 coins of which over 1,000 are housed in the Castle Museum in Norwich. The hoard contains nine coins of Carausius and terminates with two of Allectus. Over one thousand of the coins were issues dated between 251 and 273, with 840 of these being Gallic Empire issues.

Lilly Horn, Gloucestershire First reported in the Numismatic Chronicle, (N.C. Series 1. Vol.V. 1845), this hoard is extremely similar in content to that from Holt (above). The 1,223 coins conclude with seven of Carausius and one of Allectus, and the bulk of the hoard is again from the Gallic Empire.

Group C2
There are only two well-reported hoards in this group. The hoards consist of predominantly British Empire issues, terminating with coins of Allectus.

Colchester, Essex Although known as the Colchester Hoard, there has never been any claim that this hoard was found within Colchester itself. The word of mouth report given by the finder was that it had been found whilst rebuilding an old wall a few miles away from Colchester (Baldwin 1930). Such an imprecise description of find spot must lead to some suspicion as to the validity of the claims made. Only twenty-seven of the two hundred and ninety eight coins reported were not of either Carausius or Allectus.

The condition and style of the coins is such that a

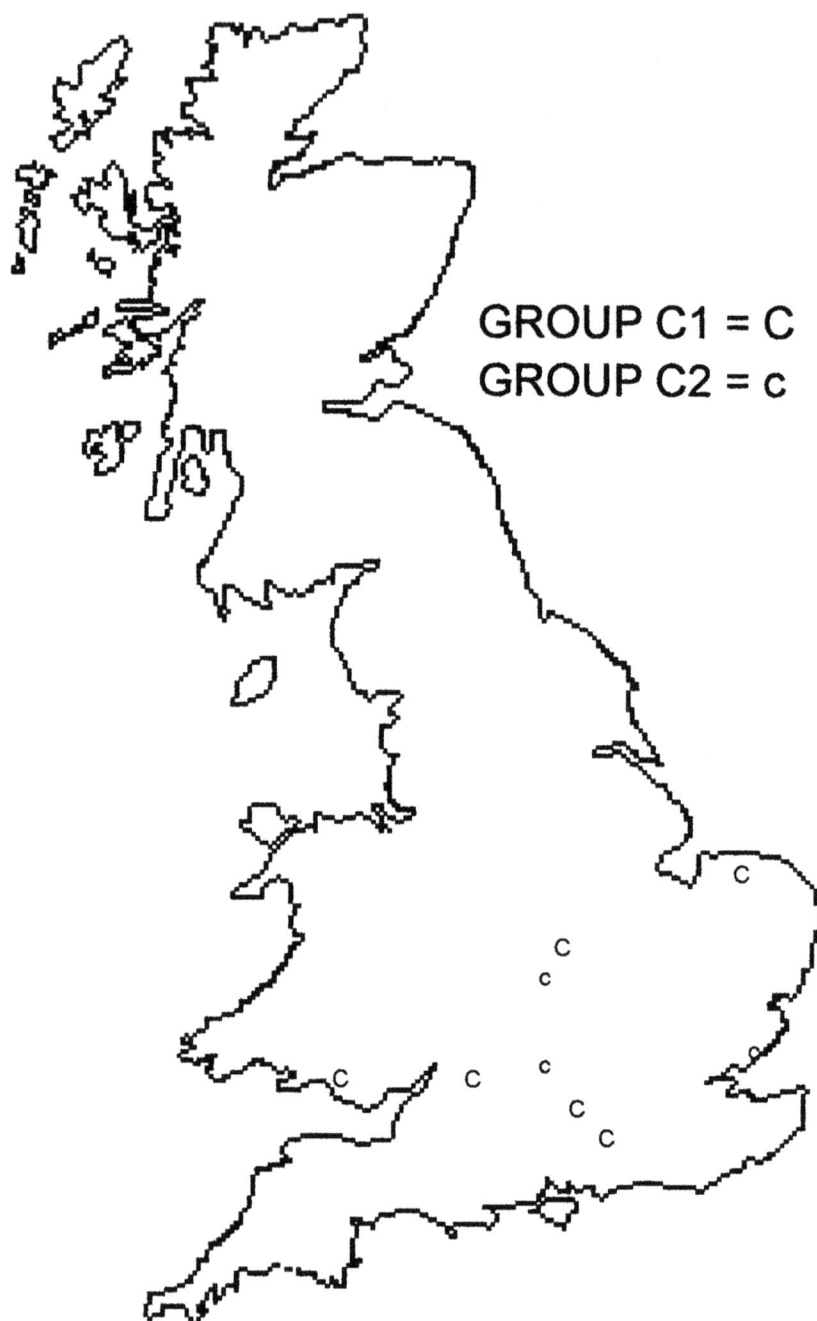

GROUP C1 = C
GROUP C2 = c

FIGURE 22 MAP OF GROUP C HOARDS

comparison of the motives of the hoarder with that of the assembler of the "1987" Hoard is not unreasonable, though the latter hoard was said to contain no coins of Allectus. The content of the Carausian element of the hoard is unusual in that it only contains four unmarked coins in a total of one hundred and two pieces.

Burton Latimer, Northants   The hoard was originally said to have consisted of between 124 and 140 coins of which 108 were described by Bland (Bland1985). Bland

remarks on the close parallel with the Colchester Hoard, (above). As with the Colchester Hoard a very small proportion of the Carausian coins are unmarked, only three out of fifty nine.

Class C1/C2
Watchfield, Berkshire This small hoard terminating with Allectus was first reported in the Numismatic Chronicle, 1907. Of the twenty three coins in the hoard, six were of Carausius and six of Allectus.

FIGURE 23 MAP OF 'LEGITIMIST' HOARDS

Class D (The Legitimist Hoards)
This somewhat enigmatic group of hoards was first referred to as "legitimist" by A.S. Robertson (Robertson 1949). The hoards consist predominantly of coins struck under the Central Empire after the reform of Aurelian. Coins of these issues, though common on the continent, are far from so in Britain indicating a very low supply of fresh reformed coin into the province. These legitimist hoards contain a minimal representation of coins of British or Gallic Emperors, and as such must have been well-sorted by their secreteurs. The hoards do, however, all contain coins issued by Carausius in the names of Diocletian and Maximian, these specimens obviously deceiving the assembler of the hoard. Details of the hoards are outlined below. The hoard from Evenly in Northamptonshire is not considered here although Shiel included it for consideration (Shiel 1977), since its discovery in 1822 and subsequent first reporting in 1855, (N.C. Series 1. Vol XV., 1855) leave some doubts in the way of accuracy. There are, however, five well-attested

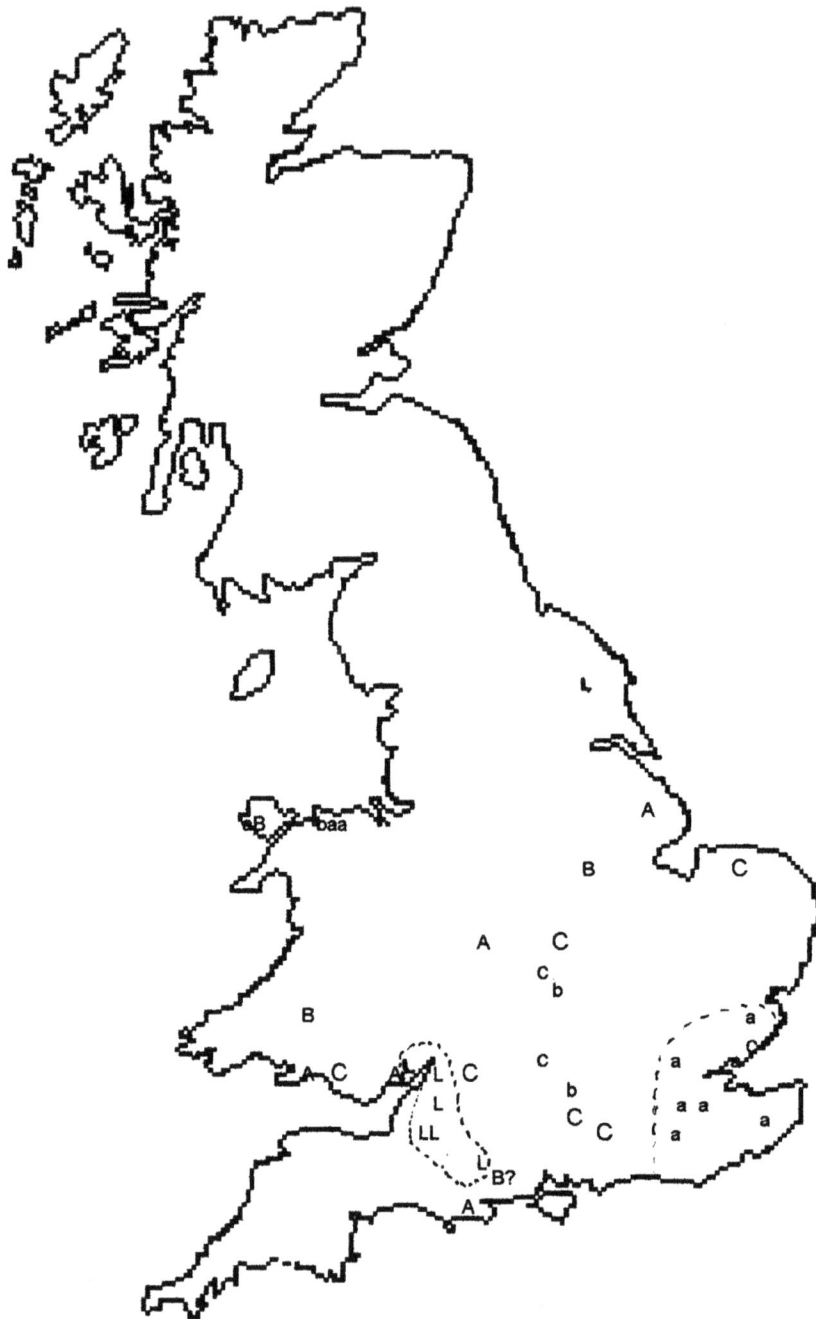

GROUP A1 = A   GROUP B1 = B   GROUP C1 = C

GROUP A2 = a   GROUP B2 = b   GROUP C2 = c

LEGITIMIST HOARDS = L

FIGURE 24 MAP OF HOARDS OF ALL GROUPS

legitimist hoards, details of which are taken from Bland (Bland 1992).

Cadbury, Somerset   Thirty seven coins, terminating with one of Carausius, and two of Carausius in the name of Diocletian/Maximian,of which 28 are central empire in the range Aurelian-Diocletian.

Cheddar, Somerset   Ninety nine coins, terminating with seven of Carausius, all in the name of Diocletian/ Maximian, eighty two being of central empire in the range Aurelian-Diocletian.

East Harnham, Wiltshire   3938 coins, terminating with 46 of Carausius in the name of Diocletian Maximian. This hoard is slightly unusual since only 650 coins are from the range Aurelian-Diocletian, but 3232 are from the range Valerian-Quintillus, with only 10 Gallic Empire issues present.

Gloucester, Gloucestershire   This large hoard containing 15552 coins terminates with two antoniniani of Allectus. There are twenty coins in the name of Carausius, and a further sixteen issued by him in the name of Diocletian/Maximian. 15446 of the coins are from the range Aurelian-Diocletian.

Lacock, Wiltshire (Bland 1992) This hoard consists of 93 coins, of which 75 are identifiable. 58 of the coins are in the range Aurelian-Diocletian, one is in the name of Carausius and eight issued by Carausius in the name of Diocletian/Maximian. The hoard terminates with one antoninianus of Allectus.

The geographical proximity of these five hoards is of interest. The temptation to regard all five as contemporary, within a period of maybe a few months,

can only be realised by accepting the possibility that they were buried in the period of uncertainty that greeted the usurpation of Allectus, and that there were insufficient Allectan coins in circulation to invade the first three hoards described. As Bland observes, "they certainly do show that some people who put together coin hoards in the 290's", notably in the West of England, "were careful to discriminate against coins of the British or Gallic emperors." Whether or not this was a deliberate policy of local officialdom in this one specific area of Britain remains open to question.

Two recent hoards are even more enigmatic. The large hoard from *Rogiet, Monmouthshire, 1998* (Besly, 2001), contains 3778 coins. It shows many of the expected traits of a legitimist hoard, but also contains, alongside types of the Central Empire, a minor element of Carausian and Allectan material which appears to be sorted for its high quality. It also contains a significant number, 748, of the 'galley type' small radiate pieces of Allectus. This represents the largest accumulation of these pieces ever found.

The Langtoft Hoard A 2000 (Abdy 2003) is even more surprising. It was found in East Yorkshire, far from the geographical cluster of the other Legitimist Hoards. Its deposition date is likely to be as late as 305. It is extremely unusual as it combines 578 radiates and 'denarii', all but four being of the Central Empire, with 398 large nummi struck after Diocletian's reform of the coinage.

Abdy sees this unusual mix as being evidence for the continued use of radiates after the reform of Diocletian (Abdy 2002). It is, however, so unusual to encounter such a combination in Britain, that one is left to wonder if it is in essence merely a mix of two separate accumulations.

Chapter Nine

Aspects of the Coinage

Several aspects of the coinage are worthy of further consideration in the light of new types which have appeared over recent years. The variety of coin types issued by Carausius is extensive, and it is anticipated that many more interesting varieties will surface in forthcoming years.

THE OBVERSE LEGENDS

The obverse legends employed on the coinage by the majority of late third century emperors and usurpers during the second century, usually tend to form a logical pattern which develops throughout the reign. The analysis of the Cunetio Hoard (Besly and Bland 1983) clearly emphasises this. The pattern used by Carausius does not, on the surface, appear to be quite as straightforward as one might hope, but it is likely that a feature of such importance, on the coinage, would be underpinned by some form of logical progression.

Webb (Webb 1933) compiled a table of occurrences of some of the more common legends, while Carson (Carson 1971) attempted to tie in the obverse legends with his proposed order of sequence marks.

The more common obverse legends fall into the following legend types:-

Those beginning....

IMPCARAVSIVS.......	(A)
IMPCCARAVSIVS........	(B)
IMPCMCARAVSIVS.....	(C)

and those ending...

....CARAVSIVSAVG	(1)
....CARAVSIVSPFAVG	(2)
....CARAVSIVSPAVG	(3)

This notation, outlined above, generates a simple system for describing the various combinations that give rise to some of the more common legends, in terms of a letter-figure combination. For example the legend *IMPCARAVSIVSPFAVG* may be simply ascribed as legend A2 (Plate 6 Nos.1-2).

Carson (Carson 1971) suggests that the *IMPCCARAVSIVS..* legends were introduced around 291-2, after the uneasy peace with Maximian and Diocletian had been drawn up. This suggestion now needs reappraisal.

Casey (Burnett and Casey 1985) points out that this legend is almost invariably used at Rouen, and that Rouen coins appear in both Croydon and Little Orme Hoards, both of which are early. This evidence has since

been complemented by both the Normanby and Dorchester Hoards both containing Rouen pieces. It is thus now relatively certain, with the reasoning put forward elsewhere in this work, that these Rouen coins comprise the earliest coinage of the reign, and that Carausius had taken the title *Caesar*, assuming that is what the *C* stands for, on his succession.

Both the Normanby Hoard (Bland and Burnett 1989) and the Dorchester Hoard (King forthcoming) contain coins of British manufacture, apparently regular and stylistically from early in the reign, which begin their obverse legend *IMPCCARAVSIVS...* The former contains four such specimens and the latter two, all coins in question being unmarked. It is thus probable that the *IMPCCARAVSIVS...* legend was used at Rouen and also on some of the earliest British productions.

For some reason, this legend seems to have been dropped shortly after the regime became established in Britain, with the beginning of the legend reverting to *IMPCARAVSIVS...* Recently a previously unrecorded coin has yielded the previously unrecorded legend *IMPCARAVSIVSCPFAVG*, though the displacement of the *C* to a position after the Emperor's name asks further questions (Plate 5 Nos.19-20). *C*, if it were to represent *Caesar* would normally be expected to appear immediately after *IMP*, and it should be considered that this *C*, inserted before the *Pivs Felix* epithets may represent another title. The coin is of good style and exhibits a *VICTORIA AVG* reverse legend, showing a figure of Victory advancing left. A further example, struck from the same dies, has recently come to light, confirming that the type bears no exergual mark.

The possibility must exist that the title of *Caesar* may have been transferred to an elected successor, possibly a son of Carausius, referred to on the *PRINCIPI IVVENTVTIS* and *CONIVGE AVG* coins, both of which were produced about this time and are discussed more fully later in this chapter.

The beginning of the standard obverse legend on coins of British manufacture, for the first part of the reign, thus changes to *IMPCARAVSIVS....*, this remaining as the most common form, until perhaps the latter part of 290 according to the newly proposed chronology (*q.v.*).

The reversion to the standard legend beginning *IMPCCARAVSIVS* at the *L* mint, coincides with the production of issues bearing the *B/E/MLXXI* index marks. This version then becomes the standard for the latter part of the reign. Since about half those coins bearing

B/E/MLXXI marks show the later version of obverse legend, it would seem reasonable to suppose that the actual change took place somewhere near the middle of the period in which these index marks were current.

This change at the *L* mint appears to be quite sudden. For some reason, Carausius re-adopts the title of Caesar. Possibilities may either be construed that it is a result of the `Peace' treaty with Diocletian and Maximian (Carson 1971), or alternatively due to the death or removal of the emperor's elected successor.

By this stage in the reign the *antoninianus* had become regularly struck on well-formed and larger flans. The production of the completely unmarked issues appears to stop about this time. On stylistic grounds, however, those scarce unmarked coins with the legend beginning *IMPCMCARAVSIVS...* fit in well with this period, and though their issue is short-lived, it seems quite likely that they were produced about this time as possibly the penultimate issues that have reverses totally devoid of index marks. A final issue of totally unmarked coins bearing the legend *IMPCCARAVSIVS....*, and being stylistically in keeping with this later coinage, does seem to exist though specimens are rare.

The endings of the obverse legends are in general typical of those used by other late third century emperors. The most common ending being...*CARAVSIVSPFAVG*, for Pius Felix Augustus. Sometimes the F is omitted and sometimes the ending is further shortened to....*CARAVSIVSAVG*. Although Webb (Webb 1933), quotes legends ending.....*AV* as a separate entity it is more likely that they just represent the errors of engravers who have misjudged the space available. It is worth noting, with reference to this observation, that a coin in Leeds City Museum possesses the legend *MPCARAVSIVSPFAVG*, with no room available for the *I*, indicating that the engraver had probably worked backwards from the end of the legend in this particular case.

The ending sometimes includes an allusion to the title *Invictus* taken by the emperor during his reign. A coin in the Royal Mint Museum, No.R56, (Hocking 1906), bears the legend *IMPCCARAVSIVS PFINV_AVG*. The coin carries a sequence mark of *S/P/C* and the reverse legend *PROVID AVGGG*, perhaps a reflection of the invincibility felt by Carausius after repulsing the attempted invasion from the continent, and successful conclusion of peace `terms'. Some *S/C/* and *S/P* coins bearing no exergual mark also echo these sentiments with a legends reading either *IMPC CARAVSIVSPFIAVG* or/ *IMPCCARAVSIVSPFINAVG* (Plate 4 No.15). A coin of contemporay appearance,but with obscure mintmarks and bearing the previously unrecorded version *IMPCCARAVSIVSPIFAVG* is also illustrated (Plate 4 No.16).

The above should not, however, be used to surmise that

Carausius first adopted the *Invictvs* title sometime during the latter half of his reign. There exist coins of early style, both unmarked and index-marked *ML*, originating from the early part of the reign, that bear the legend *IMPCARAVSIVSPFIN AVG*. One early issue from the Dorchester Hoard (King forthcoming) bears the unusual legend *IMPCARAVSIVSPFIAVGV*. Unmarked coins of earlier style sometimes carry the legend *IMP CARAVSIVSPIAVG*, where the *I* is sufficiently well-formed to indicate that it was a deliberate engraving, not merely an unbarred *F*. It thus seems likely that the *Invictus* epithet was used near the start of the reign, then fell out of normal usage, before being resurrected in the latter part of the period under discussion.

Although the most informative obverse legends, such as *IMPCMAVM CARAVSIVSPAVG* (Plate 4 No.17) emanate from the *C* mint, an unmarked coin with the obverse legend *IMPMAVRCARAVSIVSAVG*, R.I.C.1053, is also listed, but the present-day location of this particular coin remains elusive, and its is existence as evidence for such informative issues being produced in conjunction with unmarked reverses must be questioned. A late unmarked issue is illustrated here, however, bearing the expanded legend *IMPCMACARAVSIVSPFAVG* (Plate 4 No.18).

Armoured-bust issues of Carausius often have legends of very different types, such as *CARAVSIVSAVG*, *VIRTVSCARAVSI* (Plate 6 Nos.7-8) or *VICTORIA CARAVSI* (Plate 3 No.11), but such issues are exceptional and thus less likely to conform to any standard pattern. Both in style and legend these issues seem to rely heavily on the coinage of Probus as prototypes.

In general terms, the obverse legends across the whole spectrum of the coinage seem to be executed with much care. Errors in literacy which sometimes manifest themselves on the reverses are rare. This is, in all probability, a reflection of the importance of the promotion of the Emperor and his titles to the coin-handling populace.

A survey was carried out on the relative occurrences on the unmarked coinage of the more common types of obverse legend. This gives a clear picture of the relative abundance of each legend during the earlier part of the reign when the unmarked coinage appears to have been produced. In order to create a sound and representative sample, the following criteria were observed. Site coins were chosen rather than coins from museum general collections or private collections where an emphasis may have been placed on the inclusion of rarities in order to make the collections as comprehensive as possible. The coins chosen were all well-provenanced and came from sites spread across the country. The sites used included Chester, *Verulamium*, Kenchester, Richborough, Cirencester, Bath, Aldborough, Silchester, York, Lincoln. Care was taken to include all coins from those sites that had survived with a complete obverse legend. Many coins have only part of the obverse legend legible, these were excluded. Coins where an exergual mark may have been intended, though off-flan were ignored. Also excluded were coins of barbarous and possibly unofficial production, although this is, to a certain extent, a subjective judgement. The survey does not include the later coins with S/C or S/P in the field yet possessing no exergual mark. It is thus probable that the five hundred and thirty-eight coins involved in the exercise constitute a representative sample of the unmarked coinage of Carausius during the earlier part of the reign. The results are outlined below:

Legend		Number	
IMPCARAVSIVSAVG	(A1)	33 coins	(6%)
IMPCARAVSIVSPFAVG	(A2)	365 coins	(68%)
IMPCARAVSIVSPAVG	(A3)	77 coins	(14.3%)
IMPCCARAVSIVSAVG	(B1)	8 coins	(1.5%)
IMPCCARAVSIVSPFAVG	(B2)	28 coins	(5.3%)
IMPCCARAVSIVSPAVG	(B3)	0 coins	(0%)
IMPCMCARAVSIVSAVG	(C1)	6 coins	(1%)
IMPCMCARAVSIVSPFAVG	(C2)	7 coins	(1.3%)
IMPCMCARAVSIVSPAVG	(C3)	4 coins	(0.8%)
other legends		10 coins	(1.8%)

This survey illustrates how dominant the A2 legend was during the production of the unmarked bronze types, results being shown in chart form overleaf.

THE DATED COINS OF CARAUSIUS

The sole evidence for the consular and tribunic titles held by Carausius is numismatic. The validity of any such title must be treated with a certain amount of caution since it was not bestowed by Rome but by Carausius himself. There is no record of Carausius having received any such honour prior to his takeover and, although there is much evidence to support the fact that Carausius commanded the Channel Fleet, there is no official mention of his having held the expected associated *praefecture* (Starr 1960).

The numismatic evidence is limited to a very small number of coins bearing consular and tribunic titles. It would oversimplify the problem of their interpretation to regard them as meaningless copies of coins of earlier emperors, since such reverse types would undoubtedly be regarded with great importance by officialdom. Such coin types should therefore fit into a logical pattern.

Tribunic Powers were usually taken at the start of a reign and by tradition renewed on each successive 10th of December, the official start of each tribunic year. The title of *Pontifex Maximus* was awarded only once, usually, though not always, near the start of the reign (Sear 1981). Consulships, on the other hand were awarded on a less regular basis at various points during the reign. It must be re-emphasised here that any of these titles awarded to Carausius during his breakaway regime would have had no official sanction of authority from Rome.

The earliest evidence for a consular award would appear to come from the obverse of a gold *aureus* of the Rouen mint in the Bibliothèque Nationale in Paris (Pl.7 No.6-7). The bust may be interpreted as wearing an imperial mantle, but consular regalia would seem to be a more accurate description, although the eagle-tipped sceptre shown on similar coins of Probus, 276-82, is missing.

It is thus likely that any consulship reflected on the earliest British coins would be that indicated by the Rouen *aureus*. Two such coins, of obviously early style, are recorded (Pl.7 Nos.2-5). Though neither bears a full legend, in combination they yield a likely reverse inscription of *CO(SV)L III*, referring to the third consulship of Carausius. If, as seems more than likely, these coins are amongst the earliest British productions, and contemporary with the Rouen *aureus*, then the first two consulships held by Carausius must have, almost certainly, been suffinct. This coin type is almost certainly that referred to by Akerman (No.33) and Stukeley, but misread as *COS IIII* (Akerman 1834).

A coin from the '1987' Hoard gives a reverse legend of *PMTRPIIIICPP* and may be thought to refer to a fourth Tribunic Power (Pl.7 Nos.8-9). If such an argument holds then the reasoning put forward that such a coin could not have been issued before December 288 would seem valid (Bland and Burnett 1988). This could then be used to infer that the C mark was used until well into the reign, and also that the Normanby Hoard was not deposited until c.290 (Bland and Burnett *ibid*).

In the light of the *CO(SV)L III* coin described above, and the low and likely early Carausian content of the Normanby Hoard, the interpretation of this second coin may need reassessment. Alföldi in his studies of Valerian and Gallienus (Alföldi 1940), made several suggestions as to the nature of unorthodox dated inscriptions of those emperors. Some are obviously engraver's errors, but others he felt to be due to abnormal systems of reckoning. He suggested that sometimes the number of the Tribunic Power was omitted, and that the consulship number was placed before the *COS*, thus he suggested that a coin reading *TRPVIICOS* should be interpreted as *TRPCOSVII*. Though Alföldi's original work, applied to Valerian and Gallienus contained some errors (King 1993), it is nevertheless interesting to postulate the effect of such an unorthodox system on the dated coins of Carausius.

If such a system had been in operation, then the coin described above could be reinterpreted as *PM TRP COS IIII PP*, and as such would be re-attributed to late 287, a year after the earlier consular issue. Such a dating would be extremely attractive on two counts. Firstly it would not indicate that the C mark remained in operation to a later date than previously thought, and secondly it would confirm the concealment of the Normanby Hoard as being very early in the reign, especially if one considers that the coin noted above may have been issued towards

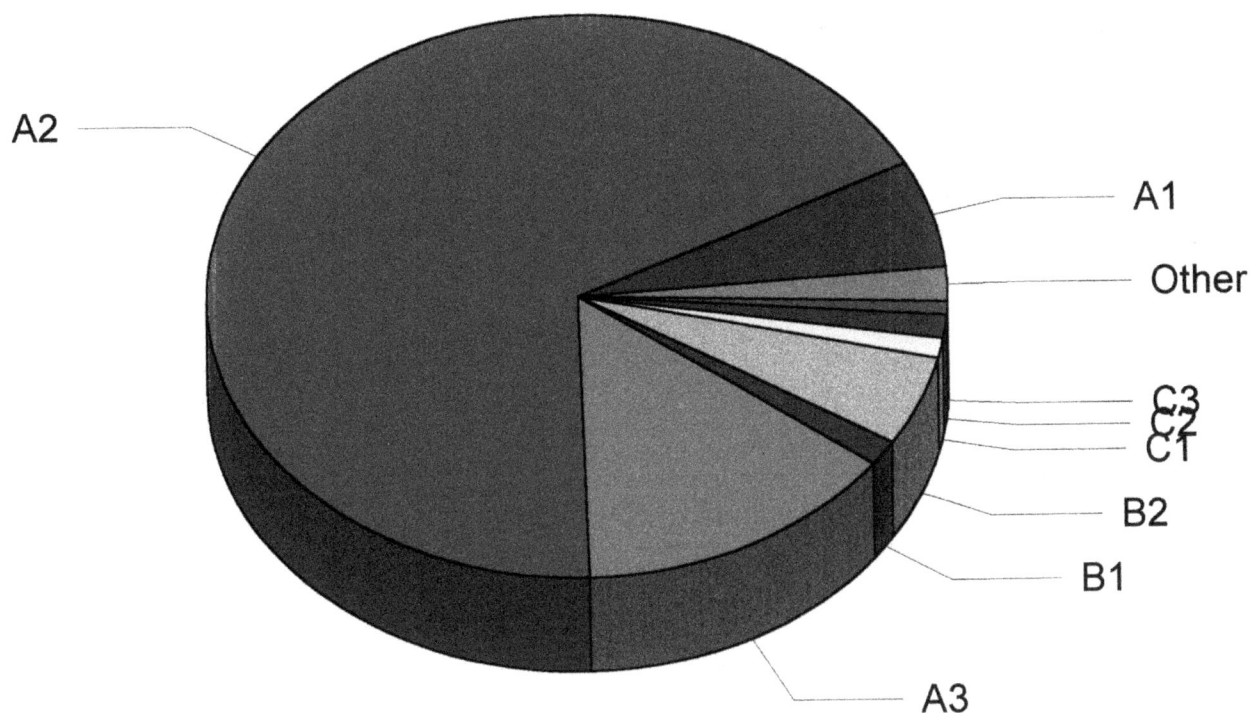

FIGURE 25 CHART OF OBVERSE LEGENDS

the end of the term of use of the *C* mark, whilst those *C* coins in the Normanby hoard could be from early in that term.

A further coin (RIC 393), from the Linchmere Hoard in the British Museum, bears the legend *SAECVLARES AVG*, and shows a low column or *cippus*, bearing the inscription *COS IIII*, although the exergue is indistinct, the style of the coin would seem contemporary with the coin outlined above. It may be tempting to think of the coin showing the *cippus* as being a straight copy of the type issued by Philip I, 244-9, but the *cippus* on Philip's coin (RIC 24c) bears the inscription *COS III*. It thus seems probable that the *COS IIII* on the Carausian coin is intended and thus accurate.

A second dated coin in the '1987' Hoard shows the Emperor seated left and carries the legend *PMT............COSPP* with the index mark *MC* in the exergue (Pl.7 10-11). This is a later index mark than *C*, possibly in use during 288, on the chronology outlined in an earlier chapter. There is no room for the legend *PMTRPIIIICOSPP* to be fitted into the space available, but the legend *PMTRPVCOSPP* would fit extremely well. Such a legend, on the argument outlined above, could then be interpreted as *PM TRP COS V PP* and as such would tie in with the *MC* exergual mark.

There thus seems a strong case for suggesting that the dated coinage forms a logical pattern as regards the consulships held by Carausius. The first two being suffinct, the third awarded on accession in 286, the fourth being taken in 287, and the fifth in 288.

THE FAMILY COINAGE OF CARAUSIUS

The contemporary and early sources available to us fail to make any reference to the family of Carausius. There exists no mention of either a wife or children, and the coinage remains the only extant piece of evidence which may lead to some indication of the nature of any immediate family.

It had been the custom, since early Imperial times, for the Emperor to honour members of his family on the coinage. Throughout the period coins in the name of, and bearing the portrait of, important family members, were regularly struck. Many reverse types also illustrate or allude to family matters. Marriage of the Emperor or Caesar initiated issues of *Concordia* types, often showing the happy couple with hands linked. The Emperor's son is often represented as *Principi Ivventvtis* or Prince of Youth, either on horseback, in the first and second centuries, or as a standing figure, often holding a globe and spear in the third century.

The propaganda value of a son, holding the title of Caesar, with the implication of his ultimate succession, thus creating a dynasty, was of extreme importance during the sometimes ephemeral reigns of these uncertain and turbulent years.

J. B. Catenaro Invenit et sc.

A

DISSERTATION

UPON

ORIUNA,

SAID TO BE

EMPRESS, or QUEEN of *England*,

THE SUPPOSED

WIFE of *CARAUSIUS*,

MONARCH and EMPEROR of *Britain*,

Who reigned in the Time of DIOCLETIAN the great
Perſecutor of *Chriſtians*,

Whom he was at War with for many Years, until received
as Collegue with him in the *Roman Empire*.

Illuſtrated with the Coin of *Oriuna*, and ſeveral others moſt
remarkable of *Carauſius*, hitherto not made public;

This Coin of her's being lately ſent to *France* to his moſt
CHRISTIAN MAJESTY.

LONDON:

Printed for JOHN WHISTON and BENJ. WHITE, at *Boyle's*
Head in *Fleet-Street* ; and W. OWEN, *Temple-Bar.*
M DCC LI.
(Price Two Shillings and Sixpence.)

FIGURE 26   TITLE PAGE OF 'A DISSERTATION UPON ORIUNA' 1751
There is no mention of the name of the auhtor of the work. The name *Stukeley* has been written in by hand, almost
certainly erroneously, at a later date.

64

FIGURE 27 ENGRAVINGS OF COINS FROM KENNEDY'S COLLECTION
Line drawings incorporated in *A Dissertation upon Oriuna*, 1751. Most of the coins are described as being in the collections of the Kennedy family; again there is no mention of Stukeley.

Any numismatic search for the family of Carausius must commence with the publication in 1751 of a work entitled *"A Dissertation upon ORIUNA, said to be the Empress or Queen of England, the supposed wife of CARAUSIUS, Monarch and Emperor of Britain."* The work does not bear the name of its author (see illustration overleaf), who by many is assumed to be William Stukeley, though it may well be the work of a certain John Kennedy (Stukeley/Kennedy 1751). The work deals with the famous coin (Plate 4 Nos.1-2), now in the Bibliothèque Nationale, which purports to show a portrait of Oriuna, the wife of Carausius, on the reverse. The coin, a base-silver laureate piece, said to have been found at Silchester, eventually made its way via a certain Dr. Mead, to the Cabinet of the King of France.

The author of the work, though satisfied of the coin's authenticity, is sceptical over the interpretation of its legend and reverse type. The following quotes from the work yield a flavour of its content.

"The possessors (of the coin) very warmly asserted it to be the wife of the Emperor Carausius and that it could not be otherwise, and it was accordingly sent as such to France. But the writer of the following dissertation, being of a very different opinion, has thus judged proper to publish his particular reasons and opinion on the subject."

It appears that the writer had, himself, been offered the piece....

"....neither did I ever consider it of that consequence to be purchased at any great rate, when offered me, never considering it as the wife of Carausius or as that of any real earthly person." The writer considers the portrait to be that of a deity, and puzzles over the name. He ponders over Oriuna being a Romano-British female form of Orion, and comments that the ending...una is found amongst the names of divinities such as Luna or Fortuna. In doing so he comes close to the true identity of the piece.

The actual coin bears the legend *FORTVNA AVG*, and shows a representation of the bust of that deity. Unfortunately the letter F has coincided with a prominent crack in the flan and the horizontal bar of the T is so weakly struck as to make it indiscernible, yielding the misreading *ORIVNA AVG*.

The work under consideration, although ostensibly anonymous, contains many line-drawings of specimens in the collection of Kennedy (see illustration overleaf), and there is no mention in the work of William Stukeley. The scepticism of the writer, as to the existence of Oriuna, is in marked contrast to the enthusiastic approach of Stukeley six years later (Stukeley 1757). Stukeley has little doubt that the coin shows the portrait of Oriuna and in his own inimitable way assigns a date of striking to the piece.

" On June 3rd 291, the festival of Bellona and Hercules, he celebrates his Empress Oriuna in that coin ORIVNA AVG."

Throughout his treatise, Stukeley refers to incidents and coins which he believes to allude to Oriuna, and his conviction of her existence is firm. To undergo such a change of opinion in six years would be unlikely, even for one with such a vivid imagination as Stukeley, making it more than probable that the earlier work was, indeed, produced by Kennedy.

Though Oriuna has to be confined to the realms of mythological obscurity, the question of numismatic references to the Emperor's family should nevertheless be explored further.

Even if Carausius were to have had a wife/Empress there is no guarantee that any portrait piece would have been struck. Although portraits of wives occur on Imperial coins of the Central Empire until the 280's, the Gallic Emperors, whose coinages were in many ways influential to that of Carausius, did not issue any coinage in the names of their wives. Although we know nothing of the marital status of Postumus, Laelian, Marius or Victorinus, Tetricus had a son for whom he issued a coinage, and must therefore have known a Roman lady very well at some stage. There are no known coins in her honour. The same may therefore be the case for Carausius.

Jugate portraits exist showing Carausius in the foreground and a feminine looking figure in the background (R.I.C. 233-4, 304 and 341) though the attribute of a whip, held by the latter has often been taken to indicate that the figure is Sol, a deity often possessing effeminate features on the Imperial coinage (PLate 4 No.3). The conjoining of the Emperor's portrait with that of a deity was not totally innovative in late third century coinage, since Postumus, whose coinage was influential on that of Carausius (cf. R.I.C.400, the facing portrait of Carausius with R.I.C.277 of Postumus) had successfully struck an elegant series of double portrait silver laureatte pieces.

Numismatic evidence for the existence of a Carausian family is, however, forthcoming from a small group of coins.

A specimen now in the Ashmolean Museum (PLate 4 No.8) which formed part of the Sir. John Evans Collection (R.I.C.753) shows a reverse type of the Emperor clasping the hand of a woman, with the figure of a small boy standing between the two (Sutherland 1944). The legend is slightly garbled and retrograde but appears to read *CO.........AVG*. Although the coin is not of a style illustrating high-orthodoxy, it appears to be an early issue, and as such may well be regular. This coin for many years represented the most likely example of a family representation.

In the 1970's, however, an even more unusual coin came to light (Plate 4 Nos.4-5), being found on the site of *Verlucio* near Devizes. The specimen is at present in Devizes Museum, and the details are outlined below.

The obverse legend reads *CONIVGEA(...),* and it shows the Emperor in military attire, facing right, clasping the hand of a female facing left. The exergual mark is X+, and its mass is a respectable 3.4 gms. The obverse is somewhat corroded and worn but it appears to bear the standard early legend, i.e. *IMPCARAVSIVSPFAVG.*

This remarkable coin raises some very interesting questions. The main elements of the reverse design and legend are clear, though the central part of the flan is obscure. Further evidence for the ascribing of the obverse legend came from a coin of reverse type Securitas bearing a very similar exergual mark +X (Plate 6 Nos.13-14). Both coins appear to share a very similar, if not identical, obverse die, the latter having a very clear legend. It seems reasonable, therefore, to suggest that both coins are contemporary productions from the same mint workshop,which on stylistic considerations, also appears to have produced the bronze laureatte piece illustrated (Plate 6 Nos.15-16).

Another piece of this jigsaw fell into place in late 1993 with the finding of a second example of the *"Coniug"* type by a metal detector user, almost certainly in the West Midlands. The coin was examined but no opportunity was afforded to photograph the specimen. This coin has since passed through the trade into a private collection. The second example is in excellent condition, confirming the obverse legend, and completing the reverse legend as *CONIVGE AVG,* it also yielded an unexpected bonus. Between the Emperor and lady is the standing figure of a small boy, giving the coin a close parallel to the specimen from the Ashmolean Museum quoted earlier.

In 1995, a third coin bearing this legend (plate 4 Nos.6-7) came to light in another private collection. It is manufactured in the same crude style as the former examples and also bears a +X index mark. There are, however, two important variations in the reverse design. The figure of the young boy, so clear on the second quoted example, has been replaced by an altar, and the female figure now presents a globe to the emperor.

The very originality of these reverse types must immediately dispel any doubts that could exist of it being a copy of a earlier type of another emperor. The only other instance of conjugals being mentioned on a coin from the Imperial series is on a rare gold aureus of Crispina, who was married to Commodus in 177, which shows clasped hands and the legend *DIS CONIVGALIBVS* (Stevenson 1889).

The military figure on the reverse of these coins is almost certainly a representation of Carausius, and the obvious temptation would be to regard the other figures as his wife and young son. Care must be taken, and such a conclusion treated with necessary reserve. An alternative interpretation may lie in regarding the issue as representative of a marriage of the military forces of Carausius to the personification of Britannia (Casey 1994), although the appearance of the small boy would also require a feasible explanation. The military attire worn by Carausius would support this latter theory, as civil attire would normally be expected to be worn for a Roman marriage ceremony.

Another coin, also in the Ashmolean Museum, may give a further clue as to whether or not some marriage was illustrated on the coinage (plate 4 No.9). The specimen, struck on a good-sized flan, has a perfectly respectable obverse type and the standard *IMP CARAVSIVSPFAVG* legend, and on the reverse two clasped hands and the legend VXIAV (Sutherland 1944). Sutherland notes that the piece apparently comes from the Colchester Hoard, but is not in the original listing (Baldwin 1930). Sutherland regards the reverse as an illiterate imitation of 'L' mint issues R.I.C.24-5, on the basis of the index mark which he read as *W++I,* though this could just as easily be interpreted as *I++M,* which, though alphabetically more correct, is almost as inexplicable. This minor point should not detract from the rest of the reverse design. The clasped hands are used on the marriage coin of Crispina, described earlier, and the possibility has to be considered that *VXIAV* is an abbreviated form of *VXOR AVGVSTI,* the wife of the Emperor.

The most likely numismatic support for the existence of a son or heir apparent *(Caesar)* comes from those coins bearing the reverse legend *PRINCIPI IVVENTVTIS,* showing a youth in military attire carrying an ensign or olive branch and a sceptre (R.I.C. 721 and 947-8). All these coins are unmarked, and of a style commensurate with the early part of the reign (Plate 4 Nos.10-11).

Such reverses are common in the third century, where a succession of Emperors, each hoping to found a dynasty, raised their sons to the titles of Caesar and Prince of Youth. It seems unlikely that these Carausian issues are mere mindless copies of types of earlier Emperors, and the propaganda value of such would need to be backed up by reality. No coins issued in the name of a son are extant, making it likely that the title of *Principi Ivventvtis* could have been awarded but not that of *Caesar.* The possibility could well exist that any child depicted on the *conivge* coins may have been the product of a previous marriage who was adopted by Carausius as a stepson and heir.

A method widely employed by third century Emperors to indicate joint rule, often with a son, was the use of *AVGG* at the end of the reverse legends. Initially this was indicative of both having attained the title of *Augustus* but by the time of Tetricus I 270-3, this had been relaxed somewhat to include the Emperor's son though he only possessed the rank of *Caesar.* Stukeley recorded several

67

reverse legends in this category that remain unconfirmed in our modern era, notably *ADVENTVS AVGG* on a silver laureatte piece, and *CONCORD AVGG* and *CONCORDIA AVGG* on antoniniani. Little credence should be given to these pieces; Stukeley was, in the light of modern knowledge, particularly adept at misreading legends.

Other coins with this reverse legend ending are however, confirmed, and to *MONETA AVGG, PAX AVGG* and *VIRTVS AVGG* (Plate 4 Nos.12-14) recorded by Webb (Webb 1933) can be added *SPES AVGG* recorded in a private collection. All these coins show early style with elements of 'unofficiality', and are possibly faithful copies of the reverses of Tetrican antoniniani issued very early in the reign.

It is dangerous to use the coinage to write the history, and it must be emphasised that only a very small amount of numismatic evidence remains extant. There does, however, seem a distinct possibility that Carausius did represent a wife and son on his coinage. These vaguest of numismatic references are only present on the earliest coinage, indicating that if ever such existed, they may well have died or been removed from influence within a very short time.

THE LEGIONARY COINS OF CARAUSIUS

Those coins of Carausius that make reference on their reverse types to Legions of the Roman Army form an important though not plentiful part of the coinage.

Attempts have been made, notably by Webb (Webb 1933) and Oman (Oman 1924), to gain a perspective of the motives behind the issue of such a series. A reassessment of this earlier work is now called for.

Webb, both in his earlier work, (Webb1908), and in R.I.C. Vii, includes in his list coins that may have been misread or misreported in earlier years. He is the first to recognise this problem and admits that *LEG III* (a lion), *LEG VIII IN* (a Ram), and *LEGXX(I)* (Neptune), though reported and listed are in all probability misreadings of *LEG IIII* (Plate 5 No.4), *LEG I MIN* (Plate 5 No.2), and *LEG XXX* (Plate 5 No.12), respectively. The gold aureus of the RSR mint reported to Cohen (Cohen 1885) has not been seen since, and must also be regarded with great suspicion.

The table of reverse types confirmed by examination of both public and private collections during this research project is thus, hopefully, a more reliable guide to these legionary types. Coins where lack of exergual space, or condition, or a combination of both, would have reduced attribution to a stylistic guess have been avoided. The two coins marked with an asterisk are silver laureatte pieces, the rest copper antoninianii. The *LEG VII CL, LEG VIII VICTRI AVG*, and *LEG XX VAL VICTRICI* coins from the 'C' mint bear the index mark *CXXI* and as such are probably the latest in the group, (cf. earlier chapter

discussing chronology). The elegant reverse of *LEG IIII FL*, showing the head of Minerva over two facing lions bears the index mark *SMCC* as testified by a fine specimen found in 1988 in Suffolk. This coin shares dies with the coin of the same type from Aldborough, and also with the specimen in the Hunter Collection, where lack of clear index mark has caused it to be mistakenly attributed to the 'L' mint (Robertson 1978). There is little likelihood that such a piece was ever issued at the 'L` mint for reasons discussed later. Excluded from this list is an unusual legionary coin from the Baylham Hoard, showing a Centaur and an incomplete legend making attribution to a specific legion an impossibility. The index mark of *MSC*, however, makes it a hitherto unrecorded type.

The issue of a series of coins commemorating legions is by no way unique to Carausius. Both Severus, 193-211 and Gallienus, c.258, issued extensive series commemorating legions serving along the Rhine-Danube frontiers. Victorinus, 268-70, a usurper in Gaul, Britain and Spain issued a series of gold *aurei*, which though rare, constitute many different types, commemorating many legions. Of the twelve legions which he commemorates, eight were stationed, to the best of our knowledge in parts of the Empire well away from the area under the control of Victorinus. Oman (Oman *ibid*) concludes that such issues were in all probability propaganda, suggesting that such a finely struck gold series may have created the impression that Victorinus was making a bid for, or already controlled, the whole Roman World. It should be pointed out, however, that such propaganda was extremely unlikely to reach those legions that it honoured since the circulation area of the usurper's coinage was somewhat limited.

The legionary coinage of Carausius opens up even more questions. The legions stationed in Britain at the time would nominally have been the Second *Augusta* Legion, based at Caerleon or possibly, by this time at Richborough, the Twentieth *Valeria Victrix* at Chester, and possibly the Sixth *Victrix* at York. On his coinage, Carausius honours nine legions including the Second *Augusta* (Plate 5 No.3) and Twentieth *Valeria Victrix* (Plate 7 No.1), but until recently no numismatic reference appeared for the Sixth Legion, although they still appear to be based at York some ninety years later when the *Notitia Dignitatum* was compiled, (Oman *ibid*).

A type has been noted (Lyne 2001), which bears the reverse legend of LEG VI VICTRICI AVG. It bears the exergual mark CXXI, which places it in the latter issue of legionary pieces. The symbol used of a boar standing left is somewhat surprising, this being the badge of the Twentieth Valeria Victrix Legion. The boar is not normally associated with the Sixth Legion. The title AVG is also not normally associated with the Sixth Legion, though Lyne does make a case for all three British Legions receiving the title AVG during the reign of Carausius.

Consideration of this type, and discussion of whether the Sixth Legion were previously *damnata* for opposition to the initial usurpation, or merely no longer stationed in Britain at this particular time, is made elsewhere, and should not cloud the discussion of the motives for producing that legionary coinage which remains extant.

It is reasonable to suppose that, after nearly half a century of military turmoil, the Legionary system, so well documented in the first and second centuries, lay in a state of flux and disrepair. Nevertheless, it is worthwhile to recap on the likely locations of the legions under consideration at the turn of the third century, (Webster 1985).

LEGIO I *Flavia Minervia*	Lower Rhine
LEGIO II *Avgvsta*	Britain
LEGIO II *Parthica*	Italy
LEGIO IIII *Flavia Firma*	Dacia
LEGIO VI *Victrix*	Britain
LEGIO VII *Clavdia*	Moesia
LEGIO VIII *Augvsta*	Upper Rhine
LEGIO XX *Valeria Victrix*	Britain
LEGIO XXII *Primigenia*	Upper Rhine
LEGIO XXX *Vlpia Victrix*	Lower Rhine

It is possible that some of these legions may have been relocated in the intervening years. Webb, (Webb 1933), locates the three legions not ascribed above to either Britain or the Rhine, to Gaul, though his grounds for this reattribution are not made clear. All three were commemorated by Gallienus and it is thus clear that they were in a position to help out on the Danube-Rhine frontier as late as 260. It is not impossible though, that large detachments from these three legions may have been sent into Gaul shortly after 273 in order to counteract a repeat of the breakaway Gallic Empire resurfacing. That detachments from legions were sent over large distances around the Empire in the late third century is illustrated by a papyrus showing that detachments of both the Seventh *Claudia* and Fourth *Flavia* Legions were in Egypt in January 295 (Parker 1928).

It is necessary to attempt to ascertain a reason for these non-British Legions being honoured on the coinage. The simplest explanation would be to merely ascribe these coins to being propaganda issues in the same way that Oman concludes for the coins of Victorinus. There are, however, important differences in the two situations. By the time Victorinus gained power the Gallic Empire had been functioning with relative success for nearly twenty years. An outwardly stable stalemate had developed by this stage.

Carausius, on the other hand, had only just made his bid for power and was probably in more desperate need of pleasing the troops in his service. Whilst it may be construed that by propaganda he hoped to win over the legions on the Rhine, it is far more likely that at the

beginning of his reign his intentions were insular, rather than expansionist. Numbers of Carausian coins found along the Rhine valley are minimal enough to suggest that this form of advertising campaign would not be realistic (Loriot 1978). For any of the coins to reach the Danube, would in the circumstances, be highly unlikely. So what then could be the purpose of such propaganda ? A possible purpose could be contrued as an attempt to convince the population of Britain that their new Emperor held sway over much of the continent. This would have is attractions in convincing the people that the threat of reoccupation was further away than Calais, but to what purpose?

The key to an explanation may indeed come from the references to the two Danube legions. Vexhilations or detachments from various legions are known to have been restationed around the Empire during the latter half of the third century (Parker *ibid*). Such a body of men may not have been numerically large, but possibly capable and trained to perform some specialised task. Before his usurpation, Carausius would have not only been responsible for the *Classis* but also for maintaining a garrison equipped for running and defending his naval base, probably at Rouen. It is not unlikely that such a garrison may have contained a mix of soldiers contributed by at least some of the legions listed above. Any such deployment would presumably have taken place before the appointment of Maximian in 286, the act that may well have triggered the Carausian revolt. After the division of 286, the two Danubian legions would possibly have come under the control of Diocletian in the Eastern half of the Empire and as such would have made an even less likely target for Carausian propaganda. It thus seems possible that the initial continental garrison of Carausius may well have contained detachments from those legions later mentioned on the coinage. These troops would have crossed to Britain with the fleet, and, no doubt, have been instrumental in setting up the breakaway province. That they should be honoured is therefore no surprise. That a relatively small number of troops could necessitate a mention of their legion, on the coinage, would only be a reflection of their pride in the same way that war-veterans today revere their Regimental name.

Elements of confusion both in legend and legionary device give rise to a little consternation. *LEG VIII GE*, confirmed after the publication of R.I.C.Vii, (Sutherland 1944), *LEG VIII VICTRI AVG* and *LEG XX AVG* represent apparently unknown legions, but since the legionary symbols are identical with those on coins of *LEG VIII AVG* and *LEG XX VV* respectively, there is every likelihood that they refer to those same legions. Possible explanations could either be simple engraver error, or even that both legions were given new and extra epithets by Carausius, the latter argument being given more credence by the fact that it occurs only on a late issue.

The issue of 'C' index-marked coins in both silver and bronze representing the badge of the Fourth Flavian legion as a centaur, carrying a variety of weapons, is also surprising, even if an engraver's mistake (Plate 5 No. 12a and 14b).

The significance of *LEG IIII FL* being the only legion represented on the *RSR* coins is also worthy of consideration (Plate 5 No.5). The production of coins bearing this index mark was probably limited to a short period near the beginning of the reign. If, as mentioned in the chapter on mint location, *RSR* issues emanated from the Chief Finance Ministry, the detachment from the Fourth Legion may have, in some way, been responsible for its security.

All of the legions are represented by *L* index marked coins. The only variant used is the *ML* predominant near the start of the reign, thus dating the issues to around 287. The fact that all legions are represented on the *L* coins gives extra support to the argument that these issues were used in payment of the military.

Webb (Webb 1908), states glibly that all unmarked legionary issues are of London. This original supposition was probably made with intuition rather than solid reasoning. It is often difficult to be certain of an unmarked coin, especially on poorer condition specimens, where corrosion, weak striking or worn dies add to the all too common problem of exergue lying off the flan. Nevertheless the five legions listed yield, beyond reasonable doubt, unmarked issues.

The problem of the *C* index marked legionary coins is more complex. Though the issues are limited in types, they form two distinct groups, the former employing the simple *C* mark and the latter the later marks *SMC, SMCC* and ultimately *CXXI.* (cf. chapter on the chronology of the coinage).

The former group includes the enigmatic issue in honour of the Fourth Flavian Legion, using a centaur as the motif. (Coins of this index-mark honouring *LEG II PARTH*, with a centaur, recorded by Webb still require confirmation). This badge is not recorded in association with the Fourth Legion at any other point in history, leading to Webb's observation that it is an engraver's error. The centaurs on the extant specimens carry a variety of weapons including, in the case of the rare silver laureatte piece, an enormous club (Plate 5 No.14b). The variety of the dies employed leads to the question of why so great an error, which would undoubtedly have caused insult to any detachment from the legion in question, manifests itself on several dies. It must therefore follow that there is a possibility that this design was chosen deliberately.

Another enigmatic type, (Plate 5 No.13) may well have legionary connotations. It shows a well executed reverse design of a capricorn left but the legend begins in an inexplicable way as *HIR....*, it is possible though that the XXX in the exergue may refer in some way to the Thirtieth *Ulpia* Legion.

It is noteworthy that the Fourth Legion, however small its contribution to the Emperor's forces may have been, is in the light of the extant coinage, the only legion represented on coins bearing the *RSR* mark. The role played by the Fourth Legion may well be significant in this. Also noteworthy is the fact that this legion is the only one recognised at all four minting sources. It would be tempting, although not prudent, to allow a *Stukeleyesque* imagination to suggest the role employed by this detachment was that of a Romano-British Securicor, guarding the mint and Chief Finance Ministry, and helping with the physical distribution of the coinage.

All the issues discussed so far are, on the evidence of the chronology, contemporary with one another. Legionary coins with later marks form a separate group and exist only with the later *C* style index marks. In style, these coins tend to be better executed and more sophisticated, in keeping with the suggestion that they are later. They include five legions.

The coins of *LEG I MIN* show a standing ram, as would be expected, and bear the mark *SMC.* Those of the Fourth Flavian Legion show a design very similar to that used by Victorinus on his gold issue, *(R.I.C.15),* though the head of Africa used on the original has been replaced by one appearing to be that of Minerva. The mark on this issue is *SMCC.* The coins showing the boar of the Twentieth Legion show a rendition of the legend as, *LEG XX AVG.* If this is another error, it is even more surprising to find it on a coin where prototypes of the earlier 'L' and unmarked issues were readily available. In general terms the engravers employed on the 'C' issues seem to have been the most skilful and careful of those employed, a fact testified by the range and quality of their productions. The final legionary issue seems to have been that commemorating the Seventh *Claudia* Legion, the Eighth *Victix Avgusta* Legion, and the Twentieth *Valeria Victrix* Legion, all of which which bear the mark *CXXI.*

Issues were also struck in the name of the Praetorian Cohort (Plate 5 No.1), showing military standards on the reverse. These issues would, in all probability, honour the elite troops chosen by the Emperor to form his Imperial Body Guard. Such coins exist with the *ML* mark and also as an unmarked issue.

It seems likely therefore that these legionary issues form two distinct groups.Both from the earlier years of the reign. Using the chronology discussed and outlined in this thesis, the former would appear to have been issued from early 287 to early 288. The fact, however, that no legionary coins appear in the early hoards from Normanby and Dorchester, may cause speculation that the issues come from the latter half of the period suggested above. The second group of issues bearing the marks *SMC, SMCC* and *CXXI* seem to be later, possibly originating from the latter months of 289.

Initial legionary issues
L, C, RSR and Unmarked

LEG I MIN   LEG II AVG   LEG II PARTH
LEG IIII FL   LEG VII CL
LEG VIII AVG (GE)   LEG XX VV
LEG IIXX PRI   and   LEG XXX VLPIA

Secondary legionary issues
C mint only

LEG I MIN   LEG IIII FL   LEG VI VICTRICI   AVG
LEG VII CL   LEG VIII VICTRI AVG
LEG VIII GE   LEG XX VAL VICTRICI   and
LEG XX AVG

In addition to the legionary types, Carausius also issued many coins honouring his military forces in more general terms. *CONCORDIA MILITVM, FIDES MILITVM* and *GENIVS EXERCITVM* types are common, alongside the usual *VICTORIA* types. There is, surprisingly, no direct reference to the fleet on any published coin. It is, however, possible that the coin described below does make allusion to the well-being of the Emperor's naval detachments (Plate 5 Nos.15-18).

The obverse is fairly normal in style with the standard legend, *IMP CARAVSIVS PF AVG*. The reverse shows a female standing left, and holding a vertical sceptre. She appears to be dropping incense onto a flaming altar. The issue is unmarked. The reverse legend has been pieced together from the two extant specimens which share the same reverse die. Both are in private collections, the latter said to have been found somewhere in the Berks/Bucks border region. The reverse legend reads *CON COC*. The style of the coin is good enough to make it difficult to dismiss the reverse legend as being merely corrupt and illiterate. A reverse type based on *Concordia* is thus an obvious consideration to make.

The reverse legend on the *Concordia Militvm* types is often shortened, sometimes extensively so. On R.I.C.23, also an unmarked piece, the legend is reduced to *CONCO MIL*. The importance of the fleet to Carausius should not be understated and the possibility should be explored that this legend could be interpreted as *CONCO C*, a shortened form of *Concordia Classium*, the well-being of the fleet.

The object in the field is, in all probability, an altar, and flames can clearly be seen coming out of its top. Altars are, almost invariably, represented on the coinage as objects on ground level just in front of the feet of the person making the sacrifice. In this case the object is well above ground level which opens the possibility that the engraver was trying to convey a sense of perspective. If this perspective argument is accepted, then the object,

which is tapered in contrast to the usual representation of an altar, is not unlike the representation of the Pharos used on the Alexandrian provincial coinage in the previous century. This leads to the possibility that the reverse shows *Concordia* with the representation of a (British) pharos in the background.

THE PAX COINAGE OF CARAUSIUS
The coinage of Carausius is remarkable for the variety of reverse designs used during the reign. In 1907, Webb listed nearly thirteen hundred varieties in the coinage, and since that date many more have come to light. It is even more remarkable, therefore, that one reverse type, *PAX AVG*, is so dominant that it appears on at least half the bronze coins issued by Carausius, though admittedly there is a considerable diversity of artistic expression in both content and style, to be found in accompaniment with this legend.

The relative abundance of this type is best illustrated by the examination of site material and hoard evidence, rather than the study of collections where relatively rare types are likely to be chosen in preference to a large number of similar but common types. The following charts illustrate clearly how the *PAX* type dominated the coinage. The information displayed on the first chart is taken from four important hoards, and the site finds from Richborough (Reece 1981), and as such should give a representative sample of the circulating coinage during the reign. The hoards included are Croydon (Burnett 1984), Baylham (Williams forthcoming), Little Orme (Seaby 1956) and Blackmoor (Bland 1982). All sources show a consistent *PAX* content of between 60% and 70% illustrating just how prolific the issues are. The second chart gives a breakdown of the reverse types in the Blackmoor hoard, showing that the next most common reverses are *LAETITIA* and *PROVIDENTIA* each comprising 4.2% of the hoard compared to 67.1 in the case of *PAX*.

The *PAX* coinage was issued in abundance throughout the reign and appears in conjunction with virtually all combinations of index marks. Although Webb (Webb 1907) published a coin of the Rouen mint with a legend *PAX EXERCITI*, the standard *PAX AVG* reverse from the Rouen mint was unrecorded until recently (Bailey 1981). It is interesting to note that the extreme rarity of this type at Rouen is counterbalanced by the relative abundance of *TVTELA AVG* types, which were previously unrecorded from British mints, but are now known to exist from a single example of certain British style which is illustrated (Plate 6 Nos.11,12).

The issue of this coinage type from the *RSR* mint, though excessively rare, is now also confirmed (Plate 3 Nos.5,6). Other rare marks, *BRI* (Plate 3 No.3) and *V/** (Plate 3 no.4) are also used in conjunction with this type, though the latter is, in all probability, a direct copy of a reverse originally used by Victorinus, 268-70.

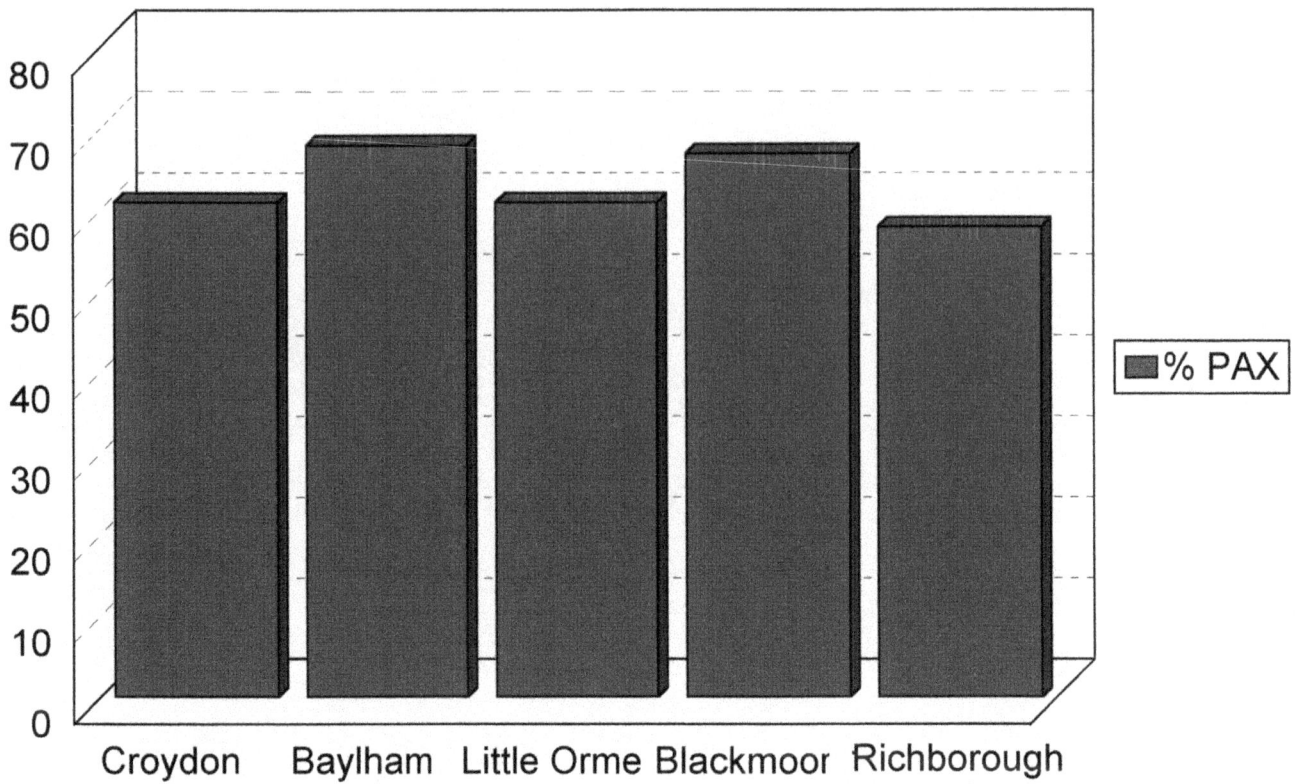

FIGURE 28 CHART OF PAX REVERSES IN MAJOR HOARDS

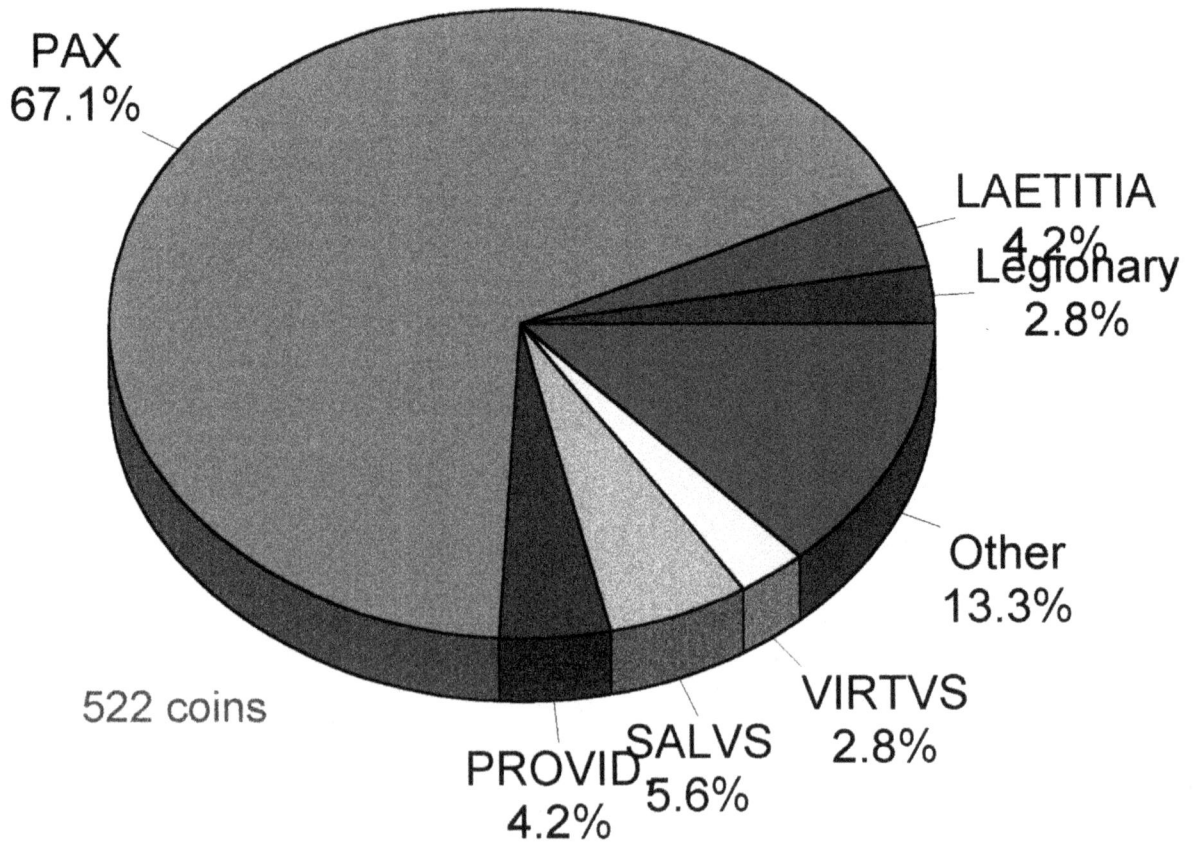

FIGURE 29 CHART OF REVERSE TYPES IN BLACKMOOR HOARD

The two standard types show Pax standing left, holding an olive branch and a sceptre. This sceptre is usually held either vertically or transversely. The possibility of the orientation of this sceptre being used to differentiate the productions of two *officinae* is countered by the fact that both types appear at the *L* 'mint', the *C* 'mint', the unmarked 'mint' and the *BRI* 'mint'. It would seem extremely convenient to assume that all these 'mints' supported two *officinae*, especially the BRI 'mint' where production seems extremely limited.

The type bearing the legend *PAS AVG* (RIC 875) exists in good style and otherwise seems to be an orthodox issue. The engraver's mistake may well link to those coins of contemporary style which bear the mis-spelt legend *PIAETAS AVG* (a variation which also manifests itself on coins of the mint of Lyons struck under central control). It has been suggested that such errors may well be the result of the pronunciation of spoken Latin in the provinces (Mann 1971 and Shiel 1975b).

The prolific *PAX* issues continued under Allectus, though *PROVIDENTIA* types become increasingly common. The reason for such an emphasis to be placed on a single reverse type is unclear, but after the political uncertainties of the late third century, and the usurpation of Carausius, however peaceful it may have been, the reverse legend *PAX AVG* would have been a welcome reassurance to the inhabitants of Britain. Coupled with the portrait of a man of obvious physical strength as their new leader, the propaganda value of the coinage would have been considerable.

In conclusion it is interesting to return to the views of Stukeley (Stukeley 1757). He suggested that these coins were issued on the eighth of October 289, "when the ceremony is performed of an olive branch hung with fruit in the palace.." and on the thirtieth of January 290, the "particular day when the mints teem with such coins." Exactly how the workers at the mints occupied themselves during the other two thousand or so days of the reign remains unclear.

Chapter Ten

Conclusions

The coinage available for study yields much interesting information. Its dual role as both a medium for financial transaction and as a vehicle for imperial propaganda makes the study of both distribution and iconography most rewarding. It is felt that this study does much to tie together strands of the historical works and archaeological evidence by using the study of the coinage as a linking medium.

The tangible evidence from the reigns of Carausius and Allectus that may be dated with some certainty is limited to a single lapidary inscription on the Carlisle Milestone, some foundation timbers from London dated by dendrochronology, and a wide ranging sample of the coinage issued at the time. The latter is extant in sufficient quantity to yield a representative sample of the types used, though even here the picture is by no means complete, and there must be many more types of major importance that remain as yet undiscovered. If the figures estimated in this work are of the correct order of magnitude then the original bronze coinage of Carausius may have consisted of anything up to one hundred million pieces. This study has entailed the examination of approximately seven thousand Carausian coins, and even allowing for other coins in private collections in both Britain and overseas, and also the coins in museums abroad, there are probably less than fifteen thousand specimens of the coinage extant. Thus the recovery rate is a mere few thousandths of one percent of the original output.

The panegyrics, despite having been studied by many generations, are written in such florid language that reinterpretation in the light of modern knowledge is always possible. The first panegyric refers to the bloodshed and slaughter of Carausian forces on the continental mainland. In the light of recent hoard evidence, the coinage attributed to Rouen is now regarded with some certainty as being issued at the commencement of the reign, terminating after a short period of issue. The interpretation of the passage referred to above thus almost certainly refers to the overpowering of a small garrison left by Carausius in Northern Gaul shortly after his establishment in Britain.

The second panegyric contains wording that lends itself to a new and far-reaching interpretation. *"....the henchman slew the arch-pirate and though the Empire was a fit reward for such a crime.."* may well refer to the fact that Allectus (the henchman) decided to make an attempt at gaining a continental foothold immediately after his overthrow of Carausius. It has previously been accepted that the setting up of a continental foothold in Boulogne was one of the last acts of the reign of Carausius. Details exist in this latter panegyric of the siege and retaking of Boulogne but although they refer to the capture of a 'Carausian' army, there is no other reason to counteract an argument that they may have been deployed by Allectus as one of his first acts after accession. Any discovery of an Allectan coin in the correct archaeological context in excavations at Boulogne would provide strong evidence in support of this theory. During these studies efforts were made to obtain details of the coins from the excavations at Boulogne, but unfortunately they did not meet with success.

By using the works of the panegyrists in conjunction with those of the later Roman historians, a timetable of events can be created which is in agreement with all the ideas proffered. This would date the initial accession of Carausius to late 286, probably at Rouen, a dating in agreement with the likely early production date of the 'Rouen' coins. The establishment of Carausius in Britain, as celebrated by the *Adventus* and *Expectate Veni* coinage issues, could then follow in early 287 (the move either having been postponed until suitable weather conditions prevailed or having been forced upon Carausius by military pressure on the part of the forces of Maximian), the base at Rouen being lost almost immediately with the bloodshed referred to above.

The dating of the siege of Boulogne is fairly accurately attested, as it is known from the panegyric to have been the first major act performed by Constantius after his accession to the rank of *Caesar*. The new interpretation of the passage outlined above would thus date the overthrow of Carausius to January/February 293, followed almost immediately by the Allectan foray to Boulogne, which ended in disaster in April or May of that year. Britain was then probably retaken by the forces of Asclepiodotus in the summer of 296. Such a system of dating seems sound and is in agreement with the contents of the early extant writings of both panegyrists and historians.

The works of the two Scottish historians, John Fordun and Hector Boethius, need to be treated with caution, they contain much information that is obviously fictional, but nevertheless there is enough accurate information present to justify not dismissing the entire works out of hand. Of particular significance is mention by Boethius of a battle between Roman forces having taken place near York, though it would be dangerous to construe this as a reason for the omission of the Sixth *Victrix* Legion from the legionary issues on the coinage. The idea of a secondary landing having taken place in Westmoreland may well be fictitious, but all the indications must remain that this would have been a logistical possibility.

Much progress has been made in the archaeology of late third century Roman Britain over the past few decades. The coinage recovered from the excavations constitutes a highly important indicator of relative prosperity. This work has used this numismatic information as a basis in trying to create an overall picture of deployment of both military and civilian personnel during the reign of Carausius.

Recent excavations in the City of London suggest that major building work, possibly started by Carausius and carried on by Allectus, took place at this time. The indications are that the work is more likely to be linked to the civil administration than to the military. The importance of London as capital of the breakaway 'empire' would have, in all likelihood, increased at this time. It is almost certain that any administrative centre would have housed a mint and treasury, the forerunner of the mint which continued production for a further twenty nine years after the return to the control of Rome in 296.

Archaeological evidence for the reduction of military personnel stationed on Hadrian's Wall during the final third of the century is strongly supported by the numismatic site finds. The indications from the distribution of the Carausian coinage at civilian sites in the hinterland of the Wall suggest that this military redeployment was followed by a certain amount of civilian migration southward towards well-established townships.

The purpose of the forts of the 'Saxon Shore' has merited much attention over recent years, as has the dating of their instigation. Portchester is now accepted as being, in all probability, Carausian, and the latest excavation details from Pevensey indicate that this site could well be contemporary. The indications are that the initial construction of the forts at Lympne and Richborough predate the reign of Carausius, but the coin evidence from both, especially at Richborough, indicate heightened activity during this period.

The numismatic evidence suggests an increase of activity taking place at this time at several military sites in Wales, and at civilian settlements *en route* to this area, such as Kenchester, Wroxeter, *Corinium* and *Calleva*. Perversely, this seems to coincide with a running down of manpower at Caerleon and, to a more limited extent, at Chester. The Roman fort at Cardiff has certain similarities to those on the South Coast of England and may well be of Carausian origin, whilst the forts at Loughor and Neath may also have been instigated at this time. The coin evidence from *Segontium* mirrors activity at this time, and the theory is put forward in this work that these forts could possibly have formed part of a maritime supply route from a base at Lydney or Gloucester around the Welsh coast with a possible purpose of supplying those troops remaining on the western part of the Wall. It will be of interest to note if any future excavations on the fort at Pennal unearth any evidence of activity in Carausian times. Such a network

of forts would also go some way towards explaining renewed activity at some small military installations such as Brecon Gaer and Caerhun. The numismatic evidence from Wales falls significantly under Allectus suggesting a redeployment of troops towards the east, maybe as part of the ill-fated foray to Boulogne.

The mechanics of coin production have been considered in some detail and an estimate of the total number of bronze coins produced suggests a figure somewhere in the region of one hundred million pieces, this may appear to be a prohibitive amount but it is shown that such a degree of production could be achieved by a relatively small number of workers. The possibility of the use of hubbing the imperial portrait in die manufacture is illustrated, and if such methods were used, then the production of dies would have been speeded up considerably. Evidence now confirms the use of coinage dies in the production of lead sealings, almost certainly used for official purposes.

For many years the relative abundance of Gallic Empire and British Empire coinage on major sites has been construed to indicate that the supply of coinage under the Carausian regime was less than that during the Gallic Empire. The inflation present during the second half of the third century, and the likelihood that Carausius would have inherited a larger pay-roll make this an improbability. Such an interpretation of site finds came about through inherent errors in the methods of calculation employed. We are faced with a special situation in that the *antoninianus* was removed from common usage immediately after the reconquest, thus the life-span in circulation of the later issues is greatly curtailed, giving specimens little chance to become casual losses. A new method utilising calculus and the setting up and solution of differential equations has been employed giving a clear picture that the supply of coinage to sites away from the Wall generally increased under Carausius, but fell in the case of some of the Wall installations giving further evidence for redeployment southward of military personnel.

The metrology of the bronze coinage has been considered in some detail, and a new technique of creating a three-dimensional surface based on masses and diameters was used for the first time. Though results were inconclusive, such a method could well prove useful in future studies. The bronze coinage was not produced to a high degree of metrological accuracy, and an observation has been made as to how much effect corrosion can have on the mass of a copper coin.

The coinage displays a wide variety of index marks. These should be expected to form a logical sequence which, if interpreted correctly, would produce a chronology of the coinage. Earlier attempts at creating a chronology have been reassessed in the light of recent hoard evidence and a modified system is presented in this work. The Rouen issues and those marked *RSR* are undoubtedly early and are placed into this context. It is suggested that those coins marked *S/C* or *S/P* but bearing no exergual mark follow on from the completely unmarked series. The modified pattern of sequence marks suggested fits in well with hoard evidence, and also seems sound on stylistic considerations. The suggestion is made that the index marks changed at regular intervals throughout the reign, possibly twice every year.

Numismatists have pondered for many years over the possible geographical locations of the mints at work under Carausius. London, as capital of the province, would have almost certainly housed a mint but the problem of the source of the *C* marked and unmarked coinages has remained unsolved. An analysis has been made of the geographical distribution of coins bearing the various marks from the more prolific sites. The results fail to show any significant variations that would firmly locate any other mint, and there is absolutely no weighting in support of the *C* mint having been situated at either *Camulodunum* or *Clausentum*. On the contrary the research yields little evidence to suggest that such coins were manufactured anywhere other than at the same centre that produced the *L* coins. That the various index marks were issued on a contemporary basis is incontestable, but there is no obvious reason to suggest that they were issued in geographically different locations. There are stylistic differences present in the coinage but this would be expected if different workshops operated even under the same roof. Possibilities for an interpretation of the marks have been looked at, and it may well be that these refer to either the source or destination of the coins within the framework of the economic administration of Britain.

This work has reconsidered hoard evidence; many of the hoards discovered during the last century were poorly documented and have been eliminated from this study. Some hoards have been discovered during the last decade, and the examination of two hoards still awaiting publication has added to the understanding of the coinage. Details of relevant coins passing through the trade in recent years have been used to reconstitute a part of the '1987' hoard which was, unfortunately, dispersed before any study of its contents could be made.

Several aspects of the coinage which may relate to the history of the reign have been considered. The few coins of Carausius that bear tribunic or consular titles seem to fit into a logical pattern. This is to be expected since the onus on the die engravers involved in the production of such an important propaganda issue would have been to avoid epigraphic mistakes. If the new interpretation of these coins is correct then it seems likely that Carausius awarded himself three consulships during the first three years of his reign, his first two consulships being suffinct.

The appearance of three coins which bear the legend *CONIVGE AVG*, and show Carausius with a lady has prompted a discussion of the family coinage of the Emperor. The study begins with the essay on Oriuna, supposed wife of Carausius and yields the conclusion that this essay was in all probability written by John Kennedy and not William Stukeley who is usually credited with its authorship. Any coins that may relate to the wife and child of the Emperor are issues from early in the reign.

The coinage issued by Carausius in commemoration of various legions is reassessed. Documentary evidence of the constitution and location of the legions during the late third century is sparse, but nevertheless an updated listing of these so-called legionary issues has been made.

The coinage of Carausius was large, and the reverse types used show great variety, it seems slightly incongruous, therefore, that approximately sixty percent of the coins that have come to light bear the same *PAX* reverse type.

The coins illustrated in this work have been chosen to emphasise some of the more important ideas put forward. Where possible photographs of coins in private collections have been chosen in preference to those in public collections which may be examined on request.

This work has been produced with the aim of linking a general study of the coinage of Carausius to archaeological and historical evidence; in no way does it attempt to become a catalogue of the coinage varieties issued by Carausius, that being the purpose of a revised edition of *Roman Imperial Coins V(ii)*. The writer of this thesis eagerly anticipates that work and would be pleased to make any relevant information collected during this research project available to its authors.

Appendix 1

The Chester 'Die'

In 1963, the widow of Dr. Willoughby Gardner presented to the Grosvenor Museum in Chester a collection of miscellaneous coins and artifacts that had belonged to her husband. Amongst this collection was an iron 'die' (Plate 1) which was wrapped in a piece of brown paper and labelled "Found with L/Orme Carausius" (Lloyd-Morgan 1981).

The artifact presumably came to light with the famous hoard of 1907, although Seaby makes no mention of it (Seaby 1956). The object, which is illustrated, has been described as possibly being a die used in the manufacture of Carausian coinage (Lloyd-Morgan *ibid*).

It has a length of 10.6 cms. (a small part of the spike has broken off) and a diameter at the 'flan' end of 19mm.. Rust has affected the object, notably on the surface of the 'flan', which is also illustrated.

Only one die used for striking Roman coins has so far come to light in Britain (Wheeler and Wheeler 1936). It is a die used for the reverse of a denarius of the Emperor Hadrian, 117-138. Although it exhibits a style close to that of a denarius in the British Museum, it is probably a local production rather than a die sanctioned for official use. The die itself is made of bronze..

Vermeule (Vermeule 1954) lists forty-six surviving dies from Augustus to the time of Diocletian, of these forty-two are in bronze, two in bronze backed with iron, and only two in iron. This gives clear indication of the viability of using a bronze die, hardened during production, to strike a bronze flan (probably heated), and produce a coin of acceptable standard. It would thus be reasonable to expect any Carausian die, especially one used for striking bronze coinage, to be made of bronze.

The spike on the object in question would necessitate it being the lower of a pair of dies, usually the obverse die, and set into a solid block of wood. Cooper (Cooper 1983) illustrates a pile and trussel die pair from mediaeval times. The trussel illustrated by Cooper is typical, but differs in several ways from the Chester object. Any trussel must have a solid collar in order to prevent successive strikings hammering it deeper into its setting. What may at first be construed as a collar on the Chester item is both small, and more importantly off-set. The magnitude of any hammer-blow required to strike a coin would produce a turning effect or moment that would almost certainly tear through the wood and knock the die out of line.

It could be argued that a bronze die may have once been attached to the flan-end of the object, since if the actual object were to be used as a die then an incuse version of the coin produced should still be present on the flan-end. Although Mr. Corbel of Jersey suggested that there is a feint image of a figure advancing left (Lloyd-Morgan *ibid*), careful examination of the end yields no trace of any discernible motif. If the trussel had been used in an orthodox setting then it would have been expected to hold an obverse die, and any engraving should have incorporated a bust of Carausius.

The actual purpose of this object remains a mystery, but it is highly unlikely that it was ever used in the production of coinage.

Appendix 2

A Roman Lead-Sealing of Carausius

The dies produced for the manufacture of the coinage also seem to have served a subsidiary function, being used to make impressions on (official) lead sealings. In 1994 a lead-sealing was found by a metal detector user near Brockworth in Gloucestershire (Williams 1995).The lead was impressed from above and below by a pair of dies typical of those used in the production of the coinage of Carausius (Plate 2 Nos 2-3). As such it belongs to the Imperial series of lead-sealings, of which thirty-two examples are recorded in R.I.B (Collingwood and Wright 1990).

Those sealings previously recorded, with the exception of one example discussed later, all date from either Severan times or from the fourth century. The dies used on the sealing in question appear to be of good style, and there can be little reason for thinking them to be anything other than official coinage dies.

The obverse die probably bears the standard legend *IMPCARAVSIVS(PFAVG)*, though the latter part is no longer extant, so *IMPCARAVSIVS(PAVG)* or the most simplified form of legend *IMPCARAVSIVS (AVG)* are also possibilities. It bears a radiate portrait of Carausius, facing right, as used on the *antoniniani* of the reign.

The reverse bears the legend *PAX AVG,* and shows the figure of Pax standing left, holding an olive-branch. Pax is, by far, the most common of Carausian coin-types, and she is often depicted holding either a transverse or vertical sceptre, though many variations exist. In this case, there is no obvious trace of a sceptre having been present, though the attitude of the left arm of the figure does make it possible that such a sceptre has been worn away by the ravages of time. The die bears no index mark, and thus belongs to the unmarked series of the coins of Carausius. The reverse is of that type described by R.I.C.906 (Webb 1933). The style of the coin-dies would date the issue to early in the reign, probably late 286-287. An attempt has been made to artificially enhance the designs of both obverse and reverse (Plate 2 Nos.1 and 4).

The sealing has a mass of 8.47 gm. and dimensions of 35 mm. x 21 mm. The coin dies have a working-flan diameter of 20 mm.

The use of official coin-dies on sealings found in Britain is unusual, though R.I.B.2411.20-21, refer to two sealings found in Richborough having a single sided die-impression, recorded as that made by a coinage-die of Trier, used under Constantine I. Some of the later fourth-century sealings recorded also show coinage-style dies.

Two other sealings, found in the Cirencester area are also worthy of mention. R.I.B. 2411.40 bears the letters RPGA which has been translated as *Res Pvblica Gleviensium,* whilst R.I.B.2411.32 is also a sealing with a doubled-sided impression.
One side bears the legend *VICTORIA AVG,* and shows a personification of Victory standing left, holding a wreath. The other side shows a figure seated, with a shield and the letters *C...AV....* It is not impossible that this legend, may, in full, have referred to Carausius, making it contemporary with the die under discussion, but its type does not tie in with that of any known coin-die.

The use of regular coinage dies to produce the sealing under discussion can only emphasise the imperial importance of the item to which it was attached. Whereas many of the sealings recorded are fairly thick, (typically 5 mm. or so), with an obvious attachment to a piece of cord or string, this seal is much thinner. It appears that the lead has been folded over a thin sheet, possibly of parchment, before being struck simultaneously from above and below by the coin-dies.

Appendix 3

A note on the effects of corrosion on the mass of an *antoninianus*

The effects of corrosion on the mass of a coin may be quite dramatic, and heavily corroded coins have been eliminated from the studies on the metrology of the coinage. It is a common misconception that badly corroded coins have 'rotted away' and therefore lost mass, whereas in practice the opposite effect manifests itself. The most common corrosion products formed when a copper coin is buried for a length of time are Copper Carbonate, $CuCO_3$, and Copper Chloride, $CuCl_2$. The relative molecular masses of these two compounds are 123.5 and 133.5, compared to the atomic mass of copper, which is 63.5. Thus any copper atom combining to form a corrosion-product forms a molecule of approximately double the mass of the copper atom. This assumption ignores the possibility of the molecules so-formed being hydrated, i.e. containing water molecules, which would create an even larger gain in mass.

Thus any copper undergoing such a process will effectively double its mass. The impression of the corroded outer layers being light is misleading since the corrosion takes up a much greater volume than previously occupied by the copper, thus becoming less dense than the metal.

The depth to which the coin is affected will obviously depend on the adjacent soil conditions, but examination of specimens by Cope (Cope 1974), suggests that a typical depth for a badly corroded coin to suffer such effects is about 0.25 mm., (coins with a thin patina may only be affected to one tenth of this depth). Cope suggests that the thickness of corrosion is very much more dependent on the nature of the surroundings than on the length of time that the specimen is buried, with the specimen stabilizing and the thickness of the corrosion layer levelling off after the first fifty years or so.

As a reasonable approximation, we can ignore the virtually negligible effects on the edge of the coin, and consider the affected copper to form two discs (the top and bottom of the coin). Thus the total volume affected is......

Volume = 2 Π x (radius)^2 x (depth of corrosion layer)

thus, (assuming that the radius of an *antoninianus* is about 1.0cm.)

Volume = 2 x 3.14 x 1.0 x 1.0 x 0.025 = 0.157 cm^3

it follows that the

mass of copper affected = volume x density of copper (approximately 8 gm.cm^{-3})

mass of copper affected = 1.25gm.

Since this copper is involved in a chemical process which doubles its effective mass, then it is reasonable to suppose that a badly corroded copper coin will increase its mass by the same amount, i.e. over 1 gm.

It should be re-emphasised that this calculation refers to badly corroded pieces, and that the effect on a well preserved coin with a thin patina may well be less than 0.1 gms. The theory does, however, justify the elimination of badly corroded pieces from any survey of the metrology of a copper coinage.

Appendix 4

The '1987' Hoard

The circumstances of the discovery of this hoard have already been discussed. The coins have been released to the trade in small numbers since the late eighties. They have appeared in the trays of dealers in Britain, Europe and the United States, and also in major auctions around the world. Many have now found their way into private collections.

The cleaning process used on the coins is most distinctive, leaving the finished product with a glossy black patina. An inordinate number of specimens that have appeared are of rare types, making it likely that the hoard was large, probably consisting of several thousand specimens, the majority of which still have to come to light.

Although no certainty can ever exist in the re-constitution of a dispersed hoard, over one hundred and forty coins were recorded from trade or private collections, that were in all reasonable probability from this hoard. Although a sample cannot complete a whole picture, the numbers are sufficient to yield certain indications as to the nature of the hoard.

Amongst the rare types recorded was the unusual reverse RESTIT BRITAN (Plate 7 Nos.12-13) bearing the index-mark C and showing Carausius raising a kneeling Britannia. The hoard contains two dated issues with reverse legends PMTRPIIIICPP (Plate 7 Nos.8-9) and PMTRP...COSPP (Plate 7 Nos.10-11), the former bears the index-mark C and the latter the mark MC. These are discussed in some detail in the following chapter. The hoard also contains a single specimen of the rare BRI issue (Plate 3 No.3).

Two coins of the later second issue of legionary types are also recorded. These are also discussed in the following chapter. One of these credits the Eighth Augusta Legion with a new epithet of Victrix, it bears the index mark CXXI and the remarkable legend LEGVIIIVICTRIAVG (Plate 5 No.8).

Forty-four coins carry an index mark associated with the L 'mint', forty-two bear one associated with the C 'mint', and thirty are unmarked. Eighteen coins are indexed S/C and only two S/P. One coin from the Rouen mint was noted, but this should be treated with some uncertainty. Although it appeared in a small group of coins on a dealer's tray, and was apparently acquired with the others, which undoubtedly come from the hoard, the patina is of sufficiently differing texture to raise doubts over its provenance. Five coins, four with off-flan exergues and one an obverse brockage, could only be noted as of "uncertain" index-mark.

The latest marks represented are two of the type S/P/MLXXI, suggesting a burial date of mid 291, based on the chronology outlined in a previous chapter. The hoard was rumoured to contain no coins bearing a reverse legend ending ..AVGGG, and none have been recorded. This suggests that the hoard was concealed immediately before the 'peace' agreed with Maximian and Diocletian.

The apparent lack of S/P issues compared to S/C issues adds evidence that the latter mark was contemporary with the S/P/MLXXI mark.

There are inherent dangers in re-constituting any hoard, but in this particular case there seems sufficient evidence present to give some indication of its overall contents. It is, nevertheless, a great loss to the study of third century numismatics, that the opportunity of making a detailed survey of this large and important hoard was never made possible.

Appendix 5

The Three-Headed Coins of Carausius

No work on the coinage of Carausius would be complete without a reference to the most famous type of the reign.

The three-headed coin issued to mark the uneasy alliance between Carausius and the legitimate emperors about 291.the issue exists with some important variations. The specimen illustrated (plate 2 No.5) cites CARAVSIVS ET FRATRES SUI. This is the most common obverse type, alluding to Carausius and his Brother Emperors. The coin was issued with both 'C' and 'L' marks, with the 'C' mark being much more common. Quite a number of specimens of this type have come to light over recent years.

Webb (Webb 1933) publishes a variant in the name of Diocletian. The obverse legend reading IMP CC VAL DIOCLETIAN.....AVGGG. The three conjoined heads facing right. The reverse reads PAX AVGGG, with the index mark S/P/C. Recently a further type in the name of Diocletian has come to light, bearing the obverse legend AUGVSTIS CVM DIOCLETIANO.

It seemed inevitable that a variant would eventually appear citing Maximian. Bearing in mind the likelihood of an extremely icy relationship between Carausius and Maximian, any reluctance by the former to mention the latter by name would be understandable.
In 1999 the following coin, reported to have been found near Salisbury, was offered for sale at the New York Auction held by Baldwin, M&M and Vecchi (Plate 6. No.19). Although the obverse legend is somewhat enigmatic, it may well be the coin issued 'for' Maximian. The obverse shows the three emperors, jugate, facing right with the legend IMPP CAESS PII PF FR AVGG. The reverse shows PAX AVGGG with a transverse sceptre and the index mark S/P/MLXXI.

Appendix 6

Virgil, *Expectate Veni* and the Medallions of Carausius

Great play has been made over the years of the *EXPECTATE VENI* reverse type being a direct quote from Virgil's Aeneid. The suggestion was first made by Stukeley in the eighteenth century. It seems hard to believe that the literary appreciation of Carausius, who was, according to the most contemporary sources, of humble Menapian birth, and of his rag-bag collection of troops, would encompass the more ethereal aspects of Virgillian text. It would be unexpected if the only quote from Virgil in the entire field of Roman numismatics was encountered in a province so far from the centre of the Empire.

Guy de la Bédoyère (de la Bédoyère 1998) has, however, proposed a convincing theory to try to explain both the RSR mark and abbreviation on one of the bronze medallions of Carausius, which reads INPCDA. In a remarkable piece of detective-work, he notes that the 4th Eclogue of Virgil contains the words..... *Redeunt Saturnia Regna,* immediately followed by *Iam Nova Progenies Caelo Demittur Alto. "* The Reign of Saturn returns and now a new generation comes down from heaven above." He suggests that these Romano-British Political slogans may emanate from a lost panegyric quoting Virgil.

RSR appears in the exergue of many coins, especially those of silver. It would normally be expected that these letters to refer to either mint, *officina* or some aspect of the administration. We must examine the possibility that the six letters on the medallion, which was presumably issued to a select few, whose classical literacy might have been above that of the average squaddie, may have held this meaning. The statistical chances, of nine letters in succession tying in accidentally with such a Virgillian quotation is almost non-existent. Here-in may lie the truth of the matter.

The original connection between the coinage and Virgil emanated from the ever- fertile imagination of Stukeley. This passage from Virgil was, in all probability, much better known to eighteenth century gentleman-collector of antiquities (the quote appears to have been used as the frontispiece of an early issue of Dryden's *Annus Mirabilis* in 1667), than to the legionary or Germanic mercenary stationed in *Britannia*. The medallions in question must now be discussed. The first was allegedly found by a boy amongst his grandfather's possessions in a manor house in the North of England, appearing in 1931. The second, appeared on the open market in 1971 with no provenance, other than a stall on Portobello Road. A third similar medallion has also recently come to light, as a misdescribed auction lot, again with no provenance.

Carson commented that the condition and surfaces of the former two make it likely that they spent some time together. I feel that this is probably true. Neither has a provenance, and the style of the female figure on the reverse and lettering of both show some deviation from the normal. It is almost certain that the medals are intended to quote Virgil, but could it be that in doing so they betray their ultimate claim to authenticity.

Appendix 7

An Enigmatic Reverse Type of Carausius

The bronze coinage of Carausius is remarkable for its variety. R.I.C. lists well over one thousand types, many of which show innovation. The style of the early coinage is often crude and erratic, but the later issues hold well against those contemporary issues from the rest of the Empire.

The following coin has a regular obverse with the legend IMP CARAVSIVS PF AVG, but the reverse (Plate 7 No.18) is most unusual. It appears to show a bearded and horned figure standing right, holding what is possibly a baton in his left hand. In his right hand is a staff which spreads into two distinct legs in its lower half. The legend on first reading appears to be PRIXET C, although on closer examination the 'X' may well be some sort of 'field mark'. Such a field mark occurs on an equally unusual reverse (Plate 7. No.18), and also on a further unorthodox coin not illustrated here. The legend could thus be interpreted as reading PRIET C.

Could this figure represent a Romano-British deity, possibly a river-god or sea-god? An interpretation of the legend is also required.

The reverse of the second coin illustrated is equally enigmatic. It shows a large thick-set figure standing left, holding a whip, with cloak flying behind, in the field is a large +. The legend ends as VV.

Bibliography

ABDY, R.A., 2002, *Romano-British Coin Hoards.* Princes Risborough

ABDY, R.A., 2003, 'Langtoft Hoard A', N.C. 162, p.390

AKERMAN, J.Y., 1832, *A Numismatic Manual*, London.

AKERMAN, J.Y., 1848, An Introduction to the Study of Ancient and Modern Coins, London

ASKEW, G., 1951, *The Coinage of Roman Britain*, London.

ATKINSON, D., 1969, 'Cirencester Coin Collections', *Trans.Bristol and Glos.Arch.Soc. 90*, pp.65-70.

BAILEY, C.J., 1981, 'Some Notes on the Coinage of Carausius', *Num.Circ.89 10*, pp.321-2

BALDWIN, A., 1930, 'A Find of Coins of Carausius and Allectus from Colchester', *NC5 10*, pp.173-95.

BALOG, P., 1955, 'Notes on Ancient and Medieval Minting Techniques', *NC6 15*, pp.195-202.

BESLY, E.M., 1986, 'The Coins', in Leech, R., 'The Excavation of a Romano-Celtic Temple and a later Cemetery on Lamyatt Beacon, Somerset', *Britannia 17*, pp.304-315.

BESLY, E.M., 1993, 'Carausian Denarii: Some New Discoveries', in *Essays in Honour of Robert Carson and Kenneth Jenkins*, Price, M, Burnett, A, and Bland, R. (Eds) London

BESLY, E.M., 2001, 'The Rogiet, Monmouthshire Hoard.'. N.C.161, p.337-8

BIRLEY, A.R., 1981, *The Fasti of Roman Britain*, Oxford. pp. 308-14

BLAGG, T.F.C. and KING, A.C., 1984, *Military and Civilian in Roman Britain, BAR 136*

BLAND, R.F., 1982, 'The Blackmoor Hoard.' *Coin Hoards from Roman Britain, Volume 3, Brit.Mus.Occ.Paper 33.*

BLAND, R.F., 1984, 'A Hoard of Carausius and Allectus from Burton Latimer', *BNJ 54.* pp.41-5.

BLAND, R.F. and BURNETT, A., 1988, 'Normanby, Lincolnshire' in *Coin Hoards from Roman Britain, Volume VIII, Brit. Mus. Occ. Paper.* pp.114-216

BLAND, R.F., 1992, 'Lacock, Wiltshire' in *Coin Hoards from Roman Britain, Volume IX, Brit. Mus. Occ. Paper.* pp.208-17

BOETHIUS, H., 1540, *Chronicles of Scotland*, Edinburgh.(Facsimile: Amsterdam 1977)

BOON, G.C., 1954, *The Coins of Silchester*, Unpublished Catalogue in Reading Museum.

BOON, G.C., 1966, 'The Erw-Hᶺn Treasure Trove of Roman Antoniniani', *NC6 26*, pp.157-63.

BOON, G.C., 1967, 'The Penard Roman Imperial Hoard', *BBCS 13*, pp.291-310.

BOON, G.C., 1969, 'Caerleon' in Jarrett, M.G., *The Roman Frontier in Wales*

BOON, G.C., 1974a, 'Counterfeit Coins in Roman Britain', in Casey, J. and Reece, R. (eds), *Coins and the Archaeologist, BAR 4*, pp.95-171.

BOON, G.C., 1974b, 'Counterfeiting in Roman Britain', *Scientific American (December)*, pp.120-30.

BOON, G.C., 1974c, 'Oriuna Again', *Num.Circ.82*, p.428.

BOON, G.C., 1974d, *Silchester, The Roman Town of Calleva*, London

BOON, G.C., 1988, 'Counterfeit Coins in Roman Britain, (Revised Edition)', in Casey, J. and Reece, R. (eds), *Coins and the Archaeologist*, London.

BOON, G.C., 1994, 'The Coins' in Branigan, K., Dearne, M.J. and Rutter, J.G., Romano-British Occupation of Minchin Hole Cave, Gower'. *Arch. Cambrensis Vol.142 (1993)*, pp.44-7

BOWEN, E.G. and GRESHAM, C.A., 1967, *A History of Merioneth I*, Dolgellau

BREEZE, D.J. and DOBSON, B., 1976, *Hadrian's Wall.* London

BREEZE, D.J., 1982, *The Northern Frontier of Roman Britain*, London

BREEZE, D.J. and DOBSON, B., 1987, *Hadrian's Wall,* (3rd Edition), London

BRICKSTOCK, R.J., 1987, *Copies of the "Fel Temp Reparatio" Coinage in Britain, BAR 176*

BURNETT, A., and CASEY, J., 1984, 'A Carausian Hoard from Croyden, Surrey, and a Note on Carausius's Continental Possessions', *BNJ 54*, pp.10-20.

BUSHE-FOX, J.P., 1914, *A 2nd Report on the Excavations on the Site of the Roman Town at Wroxeter, Shropshire.*

CARSON, R.A.G., 1953, 'Roman Coins from the excavations at Camerton, near Bath, (Part 2)', *NC6 13*, p.137.

CARSON, R.A.G., 1954, 'The British Empire of Carausius', *History Today*, pp.734-8.

CARSON, R.A.G., 1959, 'The Mints and Coinage of Carausius and Allectus', *JBAA 22*, pp.33-40.

CARSON, R.A.G., 1971, 'Sequence Marks on the Coinage of Carausius and Allectus', in Carson, R.G. (Ed.), *Mints, Dies and Currency*, London, pp. 57-67.

CARSON, R.A.G., 1973, 'The Bronze Medallions of Carausius', *BMQ 37*, pp.1-4.

CARSON, R.A.G., 1980, *Principal Coins of the Romans, Volume 2, The Principate 31B.C.-A.D. 296*, London.

CARSON, R.A.G., 1988, 'Carausius et Fratres Sui..Again', in Huvelin, Christol et Gautier (Eds.), *Mélanges de Numismatique offerts à Pierre Bastien*, Paris.

CARTER, G.F., 1980, 'A Graphical Method for Calculating the Approximate Total Number of

Dies from Die-Link Statistics of Ancient Coins', in Oddy, W.A. (ed), *Scientific Studies in Numismatics, B.M.Occ.Paper No.18.*

CASEY, (P.)J., 1969, 'Caerhun' in Jarrett, M.G., *The Roman Frontier in Wales*

CASEY, (P.)J., 1974, 'The Interpretation of Romano-British Site Finds', in Casey, J.and Reece, R. (Eds.), *Coins and the Archaeologist, BAR 4,* pp.37-51.

CASEY, (P.)J., 1977a, 'Carausius and Allectus - Rulers in Gaul', *Britannia 8,* pp.283-301.

CASEY, (P.)J., 1977b, 'Tradition and Innovation in the Coinage of Carausius and Allectus', in Munby, J. and Henig, M., *Roman Life and Art in Britain, part ii, BAR 41.*

CASEY, (P.)J., 1980, *Roman Coinage in Britain,* Aylesbury.

CASEY, (P.)J., 1986, *Understanding Ancient Coins,* London

CASEY, P.J., DAVIES, J.L. and EVANS, J., 1993, *The Excavations at Segontium (Caernarfon) Roman Fort,* C.B.A. Research Report 90

CASEY, (P.)J., forthcoming, 'The Coins', in Wacher, J., *Excavations at Catterick, 1959 and 1972.*

CASEY, (P.)J., forthcoming, 'The Coins', in Webster, G., *Excavations at Wroxeter.*

CASEY, (P.) J. and BRICKSTOCK, R.J., forthcoming, *A Catalogue of Site-finds at Wroxeter Palaestra, 1968-1986.*

CASEY, (P.)J. and BRICKSTOCK, R.J., forthcoming, *The Coinage of Roman Piercebridge, Durham.*

CASEY, (P.) J., 1994, *Carausius and Allectus, the British Usurpers,* London

CHALLIS, C.E. and BLACKBURN, M.A.S.(eds), 1985, *Studies in the Coinages of Carausius and Allectus,* BNS, London.

CHERRY, J., 1979, 'Ravenglass' in Potter.T.W., *The Romans in North-West England*

COLLINGWOOD, R.G. and RICHMOND, I., 1969, *The Archaeology of Roman Britain* (Revised Edition), London.

COLLINGWOOD, R.G. and WRIGHT, R.P., Frere, S.S., Roxan, M. and Tomlin, R.S.O.(eds), *The Roman Inscriptions of Britain. Volume II,* London, 2411.1-39

COOPER, D., 1983, *Coins and Minting,* Aylesbury.

COPE, L.H., 1968, 'The Alloys of the Large Tetrarchic Folles', *NC6 28,* 136ff.

COPE, L.H., 1972, 'Surface-silvered Ancient Coins', in Hall, E.T. and Metcalf, D.M., (Eds), *Methods of Chemical and Metallurgical Investigation of Ancient Coinage,* R.N.S. Special Publication, pp.261-78.

COPE, L.H., 1974, *The Metallurgical Development of the Roman Imperial Coinage during the First Five Centuries A.D.,* Ph.D. Thesis, Liverpool Polytechnic (C.N.N.A.)

COTTERILL, J., 1993, 'Saxon Raiding and the Role of the Late Roman Coastal Forts of Britain', Britannia XXIV, pp.227-39

COTTON, M.A. and GATHERCOLE, 1958, *Excavations at Clausentum, Southampton,* H.M.S.O., London

CRUMMY, N., 1987, *The Coins from the Excavations in Colchester, 1971-9, Colchester Arch.Report No.4.*

CUNLIFFE, B., 1975, *The Excavations at Portchester Castle, Society of Antiquaries Research Report 33,* London

CUNLIFFE, B., 1988, *The Temple of Sulis Minerva at Bath Volume 2. The Finds from the Sacred Spring,* Oxford Univ. Committee for Archaeology Monograph No.16.

DANIELS, C.M., 1980, 'Excavations at Wallsend and the Fourth Century Barracks on Hadrian's Wall' in Hanson, W.S. and Keppie, L.J.F., *Roman Frontier Studies. BAR 71*

DAVIES, J.A., and CRUMMY, N., 1987, 'The Coins of Carausius and Allectus.', in Crummy, N.(ed), *The Coins from the Excavations in Colchester, 1971-9.* p 50.

DAVIES, J.A. and GREGORY, A., 1991, 'Coinage from a Civitas: A Survey of Roman Coins found in Norfolk and their contribution to the Archaeology of the Civitas Icenorum'. *Britannia XXII,* pp.65-101

DAVIES, J.L., 1984, 'Soldiers, Markets and Peasants in Wales and the Marches', in Blagg, T.F.C. and King, A.C., *Military and Civilian in Roman Britain, BAR 136,* pp. 93-127.

DE LA BÉDOYÈRE, G., 1998, *Carausius and the Marks RSR and INPCDA.* N.C. 158, pp.79-88

DUNCAN-JONES, R.P., 1989, 'Mobility and Immobility of Coin in the Roman Empire', *Annali di Istituto Italiano di Numismatica,* Rome.

EICHHOLZ, D.E., 1953, 'Constantius Chlorus' Invasion of Britain.' *JRS 43,* pp. 41-46.

ESTY, W.W., 1984, 'Estimating the size of a Coinage.' *NC 144,* pp. 180-3.

ESTY, W.W., 1986, 'Estimation of the size of a coinage, a Survey and Comparison of Methods.', *NC 146,* pp. 183-215.

EVANS, J., 1905, 'Rare or Unpublished Coins of Carausius.', *NC4 5,* pp.18-35.

FANTECCHI, E., 1960, 'Iconografia Monetale di Carausio a Alletto, 286-297.', *R.I.N.,* pp.134-45.

FRERE, S.S., 1967, *Britannia, A History of Roman Britain.* London

FRERE, S.S., 1984, *Verulamium Excavations Vol.III, Oxford University Committee for Archaeology, Monograph No.1.*

FORDUN, J., (Bower, W.(ed), 1759), *Scotichronicum cum supplementis et continuatione Walter Boweri,* Edinburgh

FULFORD, M., 1978, 'Coin circulation and mint activity in the late Roman Empire: some economic implications'. *Archaeol.J.135.* pp.67-114

GARDNER, W., 1908, 'The Little Orme's Head Hoard.' *Arch.Cambrensis.6 8*, pp.116-8.

GIARD, J-B, 1995, 'La Monnaie de Carausius à Rouen', *Revue Numismatique 150ème*, Paris

GILLAM, J., 1961, 'Excavations at Halton Chesters', *Univ. of Durham Gazette 92*

GILLAM, J.P., HARRISON, R.M. and NEWMAN, T.G., 1972, 'Interim Report on the Excavations at the Roman Fort of Rudchester', *Archaeol.Aeliana 5 1*, p.82

GILLAM, J.P., 1974, 'The Frontier after Hadrian - A History of the Problem', *Archaeol.Aeliana 5 2*, p.13

GRANT, M., 1950, *Roman Anniversary Issues*, Cambridge, pp.143-8.

GLENDINING, 1969, *Roman Portrait Coins* (Sale Catalogue), London.

GOUGH, R., 1762, *The History of Carausius*, London.

HAVERFIELD, F., 1895, 'The Names of the Emperor Carausius as revealed by the Carlisle Milestone.', *C&WAS2* 13, p.437.

HAYTER, A.G.K., 1914, 'The Coins', in Bushe-Fox, J.P., *Excavations at Wroxeter 1913*, pp.54-75.

HEMMY, A.S., 1942, 'A Summary of the Application of Statistical Methods to the Determination of the Weight Standards of Roman Coins', *NC6 2*, pp.86-91.

HENDY, M., 1972, 'Mint and Fiscal Administration under Diolcletian, his Colleagues and Successors, A.D.305-24.', *JRS 62*, pp.75-82.

HILL, G.F., 1922, 'Ancient Methods of Coining.', *NC5 2*, pp.1-42.

HILL, G.F., 1925, 'A Mint at Wroxeter.', *NC5 5*, pp.336-42.

HULL, M.R., 1958, *Roman Colchester*, Society of Antiquaries, London

HUVELIN, H. and BEAUJARD, B., 1980, 'Une trouvaille de Carausius à Rouen', *Cahier des Annales de Normandie. No.12*, Caen, pp.63-79.

HUVELIN, H. and LORIOT, X., 1983, 'Quelques arguments nouveaux en faveur de la localisation de l'atelier "continental" de Carausius à Rouen.', *Circle d'Etudes Numismatique, Vol. 20, No.4*, pp.65-75.

HUVELIN, H., 1985, 'Classement et Chronologie Monnayage d'Or de Carausius', *Revue Numismatique, Vol XXVII*, 107-19.

HUVELIN, H. and PILET-LEMIERE, J., 1991, 'Découverte de Monnaies de Carausius à Rouen et aux environs.', *B.S.F.N. 46ème Année, No.4*, pp.69-72.

HUVELIN, H. and MOESGAARD, J., 1996, Further arguements for the Location of the mint of Carausius being at Rouen, *B.S.F.N., avril 1996*, pp.57-61

HUVELIN, H., unpublished, *A List of Carausian Coins in the Bibliothéque Nationale, Paris*

IRVINE, H.C., 1958, 'A Note on the Roman Station at Pennal, Merionithshire', *B.B.C.S.* 17, p.124-31

JACK, G.H., 1916, *The Romano-British Town of Magna*. Hereford

JACK, G.H., 1926, *The Romano-British Town of Magna. Part ii.*, Hereford

JARRETT, M.G. revision of Nash-Williams, V.E., 1969, *The Roman Frontier in Wales*, Cardiff.

JAMES, S., 1984, 'Britain and the Late Roman Army', in Blagg, T.F.C. and King, A.C., *Military and Civilian in Roman Britain, BAR 136*, pp.161-85.

JOHNSON, J.S., 1970, 'The Date of the Construction of the Saxon Shore Fort at Richborough', *Britannia 1*, pp.240-9

JOHNSON, (J.) S., 1980, *Later Roman Britain*, Bury St. Edmunds

JOHNSON, J.S., 1989, 'The Architecture of the Saxon Shore Forts', in Maxfield, V.A.(ed), *The Saxon Shore (A Handbook)*

JONES, G.D.B., 1969, 'Caersws' in Jarrett, M.G., *The Roman Frontier in Wales*

JONES, R.F.J., 1981, 'Change on the Frontier: Northern Britain in the Third Century' in King, A.C. and HENIG, M., *The Roman West in the Third Century, BAR 109(ii)*, pp.393-413.

KENNEDY, J., previously attributed to STUKELEY, W., 1751, *A Dissertation upon Oriuna*, London

KING, A. and HENIG, M., 1981, *The Roman West in the Third Century, BAR 109(i)*

KING, C.E., 1981a, *A Catalogue of Roman Coins, A.D.193-A.D.400, in the collections of the Royal Scottish Museum, Edinburgh*

KING, C.E., 1981b, 'The Circulation of Coin in the Western Provinces A.D.260-95', in King, A. and Henig, M., *The Roman West in the Third Century. BAR 109(i)*

KING, C.E., 1982, 'A Small Hoard of Carausius found near Bicester', *B.N.J. 52*, pp.7-15.

KING, C.E., 1984, 'The Unmarked Coins of Carausius', *B.N.J. 54*, pp.1-5.

KING, C.E., 1985, *Roman Silver Coins. Volume V.*, London

KING, C.E., 1993, 'Dated Issues of Valerian and Gallienus from the mint of Rome' in Price, M., Burnett, A. and Bland, R. (eds), *Essays in Honour of Robert Carson and Kenneth Jenkins*, London. pp.207-22.

KOSAMBI, D.D., 1966, 'Scientific Numismatics', *Scientific American Vol.214* No.2, pp.102-111.

LAING, L.R., 1969, *Coins and Archaeology*, London.

LAFFRANCHI, L., 1927, 'Notes on the Coinage of Roman Britain under the First Tetrarchy', *N.C.5 7*, pp.233-43.

LEESE, M.N., 1983, 'Statistical Methodology in Numismatic Studies', *J.A.S. 10*, No.1, pp29-34.

LLOYD-MORGAN, G., 1981, 'Roman Coins from the Willoughby-Gardner Collection in the Grosvenor Museum, Chester', *B.B.C.S. 29(ii)*

LORIOT, X., 1978, 'Trouvailles de monnaies de Carausius sur le continent.', *B.S.F.N. 34An.8,* pp.576-593

LYNE, M, 2001, 'Two Notes on the Coinage of Carausius', N.C. 161, pp.291-2.

LYON, C.S.S., 1965, 'The Estimation of the Number of Dies used in a Coinage', *Num.Circ.1965*, pp.180-1

LYON, S., 1989, 'Die Estimation. Some Experiments with Simulated Samples of a Coinage', *B.N.J. 59*, pp.1-12

MANN, J.C., 1971, 'Spoken Latin in Britain as Evidenced by the Inscriptions', *Britannia 2*, pp.218-214

MANN, J.C., 1989, 'The Historical Development of the Saxon Shore' in Maxfield, V.A.(ed), *The Saxon Shore (A Handbook)*

MANN, J.E. and REECE, R., 1983, *Roman Coins from Lincoln, 1970-1979*, C.B.A. for the Lincoln Archaeological Trust

MATTINGLY, H, SYDENHAM, E. , SUTHERLAND, C. and CARSON, R., 1923-1981, *Roman Imperial Coinage*, Volumes 1-9

MATTINGLY, H., 1945, 'Carausius, His Mints and Money System', *Antiquity*, pp.122-4

MAXFIELD, V.A.(ed), 1989, *The Saxon Shore (A Handbook)*, Exeter

MERSON, R.A., 1986, 'The Coins', in Millett, M. and Graham, D., *Excavations on the Romano-British Small Town at Neatham, Hampshire, 1969-79, Hampshire Field Club Monograph 3*, pp.95-100

MILNE, G., 1990, 'Maritime Celts, Frisians and Saxons' in McGrail, S.(ed) *C.B.A. Research Report 71.*

MORRIS, A., 1982, 'The Carausian era at Kenchester' *Num, Circ.1982*, pp.236-7

MUNBY, J. and HENIG, M., 1977, *Roman Life and Art in Britain, Part (ii), BAR 41*

MYTUM, H., 1981, 'Ireland and Rome; The Maritime Frontier', in King, A. and Henig, M., *The Roman West in the Third Century, BAR 109(ii)*, pp.445-9

NAYLING, N., MAYNARD, D. and McGRAIL, S., 1994, 'Barland's Farm, Magor, Gwent: a Romano-Celtic boat', *Antiquity 68,* pp.596-603

OMAN, C., 1924, 'The Legionary Coins of Victorinus, Carausius and Allectus', *N.C.5 4*, pp.53-68

ORDNANCE SURVEY, 1978, *Map of Roman Britain*, 4th Edition

PEARCE, B.W., 1958, 'The Coins', in Cotton, M.A. and Gathercole, P.W., *Excavations at Clausentum, Southampton, 1951-4*, London

POTTER, T.W.(ed), 1979, *The Romans in North-West England*, C.&W.A.A.S. Research Series Volume 1.

REECE, R., 1970, *Roman Coins*, London

REECE, R., 1972, 'A Short Survey of the Roman Coins found on Fourteen Sites in Britain', *Britannia 3*, pp.269-76

REECE, R., 1973, 'Roman Coinage in the Western Empire', *Britannia 4*, pp.227-51

REECE, R., 1974, 'Numerical Aspects of Roman Coin Hoards in Britain', in Casey, P.J. and Reece, R., *Coins and the Archaeologist, BAR 4*, pp.78-94

REECE, R., 1975, 'The Coins', in CUNLIFFE, B.W., *Excavations at Portchester Castle*, Society of Antiquaries Research Report 33, London, pp.188-97

REECE, R., 1981, *The Roman Coins from Richborough*, Institute of Archaeology Bulletin 18, London

REECE, R., 1984, 'The Coins', in Frere, S.S., *Verulamium Excavations, Vol.III*, Oxford

REECE, R., 1987a, 'The Roman Coins', in Crummy, N., *The Coins from the Excavations in Colchester, 1971-9*, pp.17-23

REECE, R., 1987b, *Coinage in Roman Britain*, London

RIVET, A.C.F. and SMITH, C., 1979, *The Place Names of Roman Britain*

ROBERTSON, A.S., 1949, 'Two Hoards of Roman Coins from Wiltshire', *N.C.6 9, pp.245-53*

ROBERTSON, A.S., 1974, 'Romano-British Coin Hoards, their Numismatic, Archaeological and Historical Significance', in Casey, P.J. and Reece, R., *Coins and the Archaeologist, BAR 4*

ROBERTSON, A.S., 1978, *Roman Imperial Coins in the Hunter Coin Cabinet, Vol.IV, Oxford*

RYAN, N.S., 1988, *Fourth Century Coin Finds from Roman Britain, A Computer Analysis, BAR 183*

SAVORY, H.N., after GARDNER, W., 1964, *Dinorben, A Hillfort occupied in early iron-age and Roman times*, N.M.W., Cardiff

SCHULLA, M.F., 1982, 'The Roman Coins from Traprain Law', *Proc.Soc.Antiq.Scot. 112*, pp.285-94

SEABY, H.A., 1956, 'A Find of Coins of Carausius from the Little Orme's Head', *N.C.6 16*, pp.205-46

SELLWOOD, D., WHITTING, P.and WILLIAMS, R., 1985, *Sasanian Coins*, London

SHIEL, N., 1972, 'Some Coins of Carausius from Richborough', *Arch.Cant 87*, pp.115-20

SHIEL, N., 1973a, 'The Copper Denarii of Carausius', *Num.Circ.81*, pp.330-2

SHIEL, N., 1973b, 'The "Opes" Legend on Coins of Carausius', *Revue Numismatique6 15*, pp.166-8

SHIEL, N., 1974, 'Un aureus de Carausius conservé au Cabinet des Medailles de Paris', *Revue Numismatique 16*, pp.163-6

SHIEL, N., 1975a, *The Blackmoor Hoard (sale Catalogue)*, Christies, London

SHIEL, N., 1975b, 'The Coinage of Carausius as a Form of Vulgar Latin', *Britannia 6*, pp.146-9

SHIEL, N., 1976, 'The BRI Coins of Carausius', *N.C.7 16*, pp.223-6

SHIEL, N., 1977a, *The Episode of Carausius and Allectus, BAR 40*

SHIEL, N., 1977b, 'Carausian and Allectan Coin Evidence from the Northern Frontier', *Archaeologia Aeliana 5*, pp.75-9

SHIEL, N., 1978, '"Carausius et Fratres Sui"', *B.N.J.*

48, pp.7-11

SHIEL, N., 1979, 'Another BRI Coin of Carausius', *Num.Circ.*, pp.336-7

SHIEL, N., 1980, 'Carausian Rarities', *Num.Circ.*, pp.42-3

SIMPSON, G., 1964, *Britons and the Roman Army*, London

SMITH, J.A., 1854, 'Notice of various Roman Coins found in Red Abbeystead and adjoining fields to the East of the village of Newstead, Roxboroughshire', *Proc.Soc.Antiq.Scot. 1,* (1851-4), pp.33-8

STARR, C., 1960, *The Roman Imperial Navy, 31B.C.-A.D.324*, Cambridge

STEPHENSON, S., 1889, *A Dictionary of Roman Coins*, London

STEVENS-COX, J, 1988, *Durotrigian, Roman and Byzantine Coins Found at Ilchester, 1927-1986.*

STEWART, B.H.I.H., 1963, 'Medieval Die Output', *N.C.7 3*, pp.97-106

STRICKLAND, T.J., 1981, 'Third Century Chester', in King, A. and Henig, M., *The Roman West in the Third Century. BAR 109ii*

STUKELEY, W., (now credited to KENNEDY, J.), 1751, *A Dissertation upon Oriuna*, London

STUKELEY, W., 1757, *The Medallic History of Marcus Aurelius Valerius Carausius*, London

SUTHERLAND, C.H.V., 1937a, *Coinage and Currency in Roman Britain*, Oxford

SUTHERLAND, C.H.V., 1937b, 'An Unpublished Naval Type of Carausius', *N.C.5 17*, pp.306-9

SUTHERLAND, C.H.V., 1944, 'The Evans Collection at Oxford', *N.C.6 4*, pp.1-26

TAYLOR, G.A., 1930, 'A Find of Roman Coins at Neath, Glamorgan', *N.C.5 10*, pp.164-71

THOMAS, N., 1760, *Eutropius: Historiae Romanae Breviarum, with English translation and notes*, London

VERMEULE, C.C., 1954, *Notes on Ancient Dies and Coining Methods*, London

WACHER, J., 1974, *The Towns of Roman Britain*, London

WADE, W.V., 1953a, 'Carausius , Restorer of Britain', *N.C.6 13*, p.131

WADE, W.V., 1953b, 'Coins from Aldborough, Boroughbridge, Yorkshire - "Isurium Brigantum"', *N.C.6 13*, pp.132-4

WALKER, D.R., 1988, 'The Coins', in Cunliffe, B., *The Temple of Sulis Minerva at Bath, Vol.2.*, Oxford

WARD, J., 1907, 'The Roman Remains at Cwmbrwyn, Carmarthenshire', *Arch.Camb.6 7*, pp.175 ff.

WATSON, J., 1886, *Fordun's History of Scotland: a post-Reformation Forgery?*, Peebles

WATSON, G., 1946, *Boece's History of Scotland, in the Mar Lodge Translation*, Edinburgh

WEBB, P.H., 1907, 'The Reign and Coinage of Carausius, A.D.287-293', *N.C.4 7*, pp.1 ff.

WEBB, P.H., 1925, 'The Linchmere Hoard', N.C.5 5, pp.173-235

WEBB, P.H., 1930, 'A Note on the Colchester Find of Carausius', *N.C.5 10*, pp.196-8

WEBB, P.H., 1933, *Roman Imperial Coinage, Vol.V part ii*, London

WEBSTER, G., 1985, *The Roman Imperial Army, 3rd Edition*, London

WELSBY, D.A., 1982, *The Roman Military Defence of the British Provinces in its Later Phases, BAR 101*

WHATMORE, A.W., 1913, *Insulae Britannicae*, London

WHEELER, R.E.M. and WHEELER, T.V., 1932, *The Lydney Excavations 1928-9*, Report of the Society of Antiquaries 4, London

WHEELER, R.E.M. and WHEELER, T.V., 1936, *Verulamium, A Belgic and Two Roman Cities*, Oxford

WILLIAMS, H.P.G., 1990, 'A Small Carausian Hoard from the Wheeler Excavations at "Verulamivm"', B.N.J. 60, p.130

WILLIAMS, H.P.G., 1992, 'Coin supply in Britain in the late third century as evidenced by a mathematical interpretaion of site finds', *N.C. 1992*, pp.49-56

WILLIAMS, H.P.G., 1995, 'A Roman Lead Sealing of Carausius from Gloucestershire', *Britannia 26*, pp.323-4

WILLIAMS, T., 1993, *Public Buildings in the South-West Corner of Roman London*. C.B.A. Research Report 88.

Plates

HUGH P.G. WILLIAMS

Plate 1

The Carlisle Milestone

The Chester 'Die'

The Carlisle Milestone

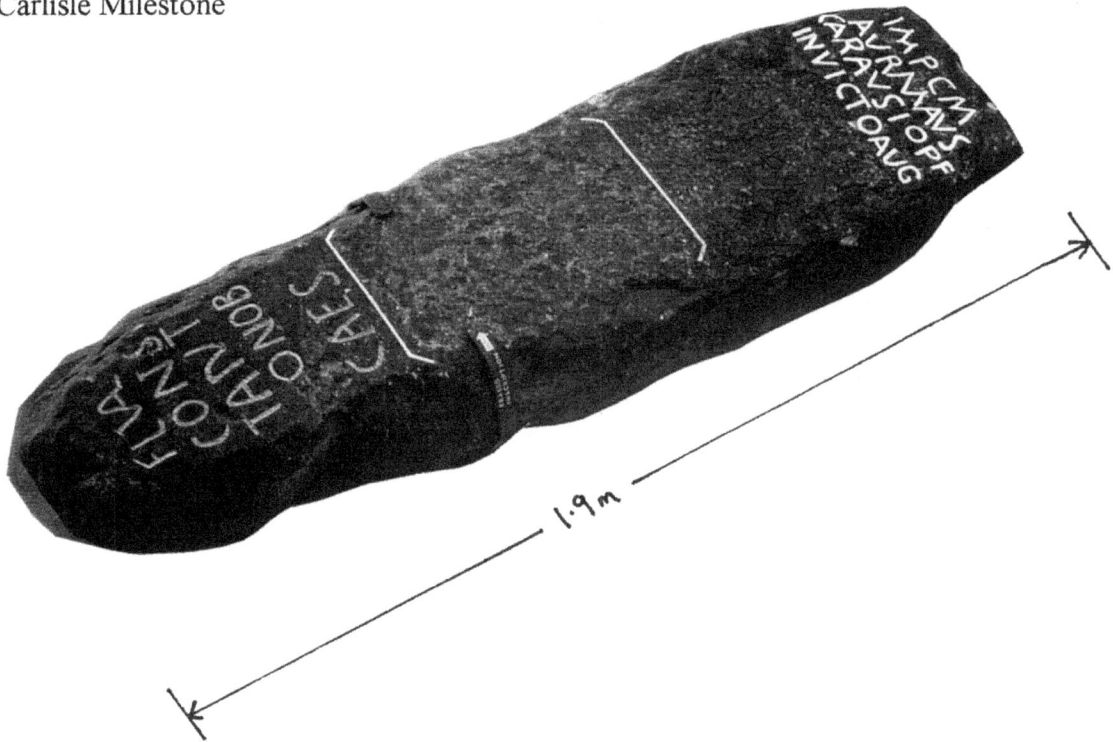

The Chester 'Die'

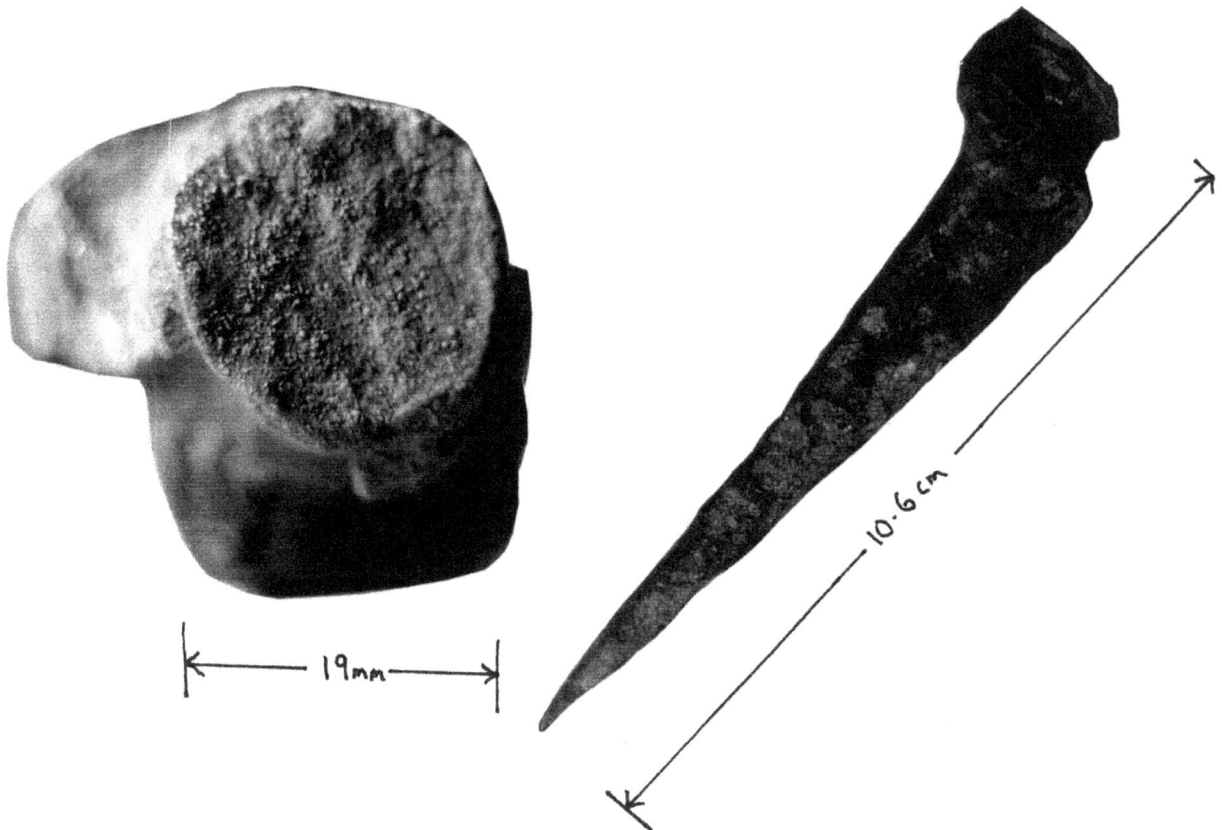

Plate 1

Plate 2

1-4. CARAUSIUS, lead sealing, obv. IMP CARAVSIVS(PFAVG), rev. PAX AVG,Pax standing left holding olive branch, no index mark, 8.47gms., 35mm. X 21mm.,found nr. Brockworth, Glos., private collection.

5. CARAUSIUS, antoninianus, obv. CARAVSIVS ET FRATRES SVI, busts of Carausius, Maximian and Diocletian jugate left, rev. PAX AVGGG, Pax standing left holding vertical sceptre and olive branch, index mark S/P/C, 22mm., RIC 1.

6. CARAUSIUS, aureus, obv. VIRTVS CARAVSI, rev. ROMANO RENOVA,wolf and twins, index mark RSR, 4.33gms., 20mm., RIC 534, Bibliothèque Nationale, Paris

7-8. CARAUSIUS, 'denarius', obv. IMP CARAVSIVSPFAVG , rev. ADVENTVS AVG, Carausius on horseback left, captive below, no index mark, 19mm.,RIC 707(var), King 8, private collection

9. CARAUSIUS, antoninianus, obv. IMP CARAVSIVSPFAVG, rev. ADVENTVS
AVG, Carausius on horseback left, captive below, no index mark, 3.56gms.,20mm., RIC 732, private collection.

10. CARAUSIUS, 'denarius', obv. IMP CARAVSIVSPFAVG, rev EXPECTATE VENI, Britannia greeting Carausius, index mark RSR, 18mm., RIC 554, King 38, private collection

11-12. NARSEH (Sasanian King c.290), drachm, obv. bust of king right, rev. fire altar and two attendants, mounted in antiquity, Sellwood 26, private collection

13. CARAUSIUS, antoninianus, obv. IMP CARAVSIVSPFAVG facing bust, rev.
SALVS AVG, Salus stg. left feeding snake, index mark C, RIC 400, private collection

14-15. CARAUSIUS, 'denarius', obv. IMPCARAVSIVSPFAVG, rev. VBERITA AV, maid milking cow, index mark RSR, RIC -, King -, private collection

Plate 2

Plate 3

1-2. CARAUSIUS, antoninianus, obv. VIRTCARAVSIAV, rev., FELICITA AVG, index mark OPR (Rouen), 22mm, RIC 636, found near Chantilly, France, Bibliothèque Nationale, Paris.

3. CARAUSIUS, antoninianus, obv. IMP CARAVSIVS PFAVG, rev. PAX AVG, Pax standing left with vertical sceptre and olive branch, index mark BRI, 5.51 gms., 24 mm., RIC -,'1987' Hoard, private collection.

4. CARAUSIUS, antoninianus, obv. IMP CARAVSIVS PFAVG, rev. PAX AVG, Pax standing left with transverse sceptre and olive branch, index mark V/*/, 4.99gms., 21 mm., RIC 121, private collection

5-6. CARAUSIUS, antoninianus, obv. IMP CARAVSIVSPFAV, rev. PAX AVG, Pax standing left with vertical sceptre and olive branch, index mark RSR , 4.67gms., 23 mm., RIC -, private collection

7-8. CARAUSIUS, antoninianus, obv. IMP CARAVSIVS PFAVG, rev. ΓAETITIAAVG, no index mark, 3.56 gms., 22 mm., RIC -, private collection.

9-10. CARAUSIUS, as 7-8 but 1.81 gms., 18 mm., private collection.

11. CARAUSIUS, antoninianus, obv. VICTORIA CARAVSIA, armed, radiate bust right, rev. FORTVNGV, no index mark, 4.36 gms., 23 mm., RIC 786, Little Orme's Head Hoard I, British Museum.

12-13. ALLECTUS, antoninianus, obv. IMPC ALLECTVS PFAVG, rev. PAX AVG, Pax standing left with vertical sceptre and olive branch, index mark S/P/ML, 23 mm., RIC 28, overstruck on antoninianus of Carausius, York Museum.

14. CARAUSIUS, antoninianus obv. IMP CARAVSIVS PF AVGG, bust right Rev. VRBIS AVG, hexastyle temple containing MVLTIS IMP, RES in exergue 21mm. RIC -. Private collection

Plate 3

Plate 4

1-2. CARAUSIUS, 'denarius', obv. IMPCARAVSIVS PFAV, rev. (F)ORTVNA AVG, bust of Fortuna right, no index mark, 3.14gms, 19mm., RIC 565, King 65, Bibliothèque Nationale, Paris.

3. CARAUSIUS, antoninianus, obv. IMPCCARAVSIVS PFAVG, jugate busts left of Carausius and Sol?, rev. PROVIDEN AVG, Providentia standing left, index
mark S/C/C, 4.28 gms., 24 mm., RIC - , private collection.

4-5, CARAUSIUS, antoninianus, obv. IMP CARAVSIVS PFAVG, rev. CONIVGEAVG, Carausius offering hand to female, below child?, index mark x +, 3.38 gms., 19mm., RIC -, found at Verlucio, Devizes Museum.

6-7. CARAUSIUS, antoninianus, obv. IMP CARAVSIVS AVG, rev. CONIVG(EAVG), Carausius receiving/giving globe from/to female, altar below, index mark + x, 19 mm., RIC - , private collection.

8. CARAUSIUS, antoninianus, obv. IMPCARAVSIVS PFAVG, rev. COMES AVG retrograde, Carausius standing with female, child in front, no index mark,
4.43 gms., 20 mm., RIC753, Ashmolean Museum, Oxford.

9. CARAUSIUS, antoninianus, obv. IMPCARAVSIVS PFAVG, rev. VXIAV, clasped hands, index mark I++M, 3.62 gms., 24 mm., RIC - , Ashmolean Museum, Oxford.

10-11. CARAUSIUS, antoninianus, obv. IMP CARAVSIVS PFAVG, rev. PRINCIPI IVVENTVT, youth standing left holding miltary standard and sceptre,
4.80 gms., 20 mm., RIC 947, private collection.

12-13. CARAUSIUS, antoninianus, obv. IMP CARAVSIVS AVG, rev. VIRTVS AVGG, Mars standing left, no index mark, 4.41 gms., 22mm., RIC 1051, private collection.

14. CARAUSIUS, antoninianus, as above, 3.44 gms., 20 mm., RIC 1051, Little Orme's Head Hoard I, National Museum of Wales, Cardiff.

15. CARAUSIUS, antoninianus, obv. IMP CCARAVSIVSPFINAVG, rev. PAX AVG, Pax standing left with transverse sceptre and olive branch, index mark
S/P/, 3.69 gms., 25 mm., RIC 487, '1987' Hoard, private collection.

16. CARAUSIUS, antoninianus, obv. IMP CARAVSIVS PIFAVG, rev. PAX AVG, Pax standing left with vertical sceptre and olive branch, index mark obscure, 5.31 gms., 23 mm., RIC - , '1987' Hoard, private collection.

17. CARAUSIUS, antoninianus, obv. IMPCMAVM CARAVSIVSPAVG, rev. PAX AVGGG, Pax standing left holding vertical sceptre and olive branch, index
mark S/P/C, 3.63 gms, 24 mm., RIC 308, private collection. (This supports Webb's observation that Stukeley misread the obverse legend as IMPCMAVRVCA...

18. CARAUSIUS, antoninianus, obv. IMPCMA CARAVSIVSPFAVG, rev. PAX AVG, Pax with vertical sceptre and olive branch, no index mark, 4.80 gms., 22 mm., RIC - , private collection.

1

2

3

5 (enlarged)

4

5

6

7

8

9

10

11

14

12

13

15

16

17

18

Plate 4

Plate 5

1-14b. CARAUSIUS, Legionary reverse types.

1. Antoninianus,COHRT PRAET, four standards, no index mark, RIC 741, private collection.

2. Antoninianus, LEG I MIN, ram right, index mark ML, RIC 56, private collection.

3. Antoninianus, LEG II AVG, capricorn left, index mark ML, RIC 58, private collection.

4. Antoninianus, LEG IIII FL, lion right, index mark ML, RIC 69, private collection.

5. 'Denarius', LEG IIII FL, lion holding thunderbolt in jaws left, index mark RSR, RIC 568, British Museum.

6. Antoninianus, LEG VII CL, bull right, unmarked, RIC 75, private collection.

7. Antoninianus, LEG VIII AVG, bull right, index mark ML, RIC 77, private collection.

8. Antoninianus, LEG VIII VICTRI AVG, index mark CXXI, RIC - , bull right, '1987' Hoard, private collection.

9. Antoninianus, LEG XX AVG, boar right, index mark SMC, RIC 275, British Museum.

10. Antoninianus, LEG XX VAL VICTRICI...., boar left, index mark CXXI, RIC - , private collection.

11. Antoninianus, LEG IIXX PRIMIG, index mark ML, capricorn left. RIC 80, private collection.

12. Antoninianus, LEG XXX VLPIA, Neptune standing left, no index mark, RIC 84, private collection.

12a. Antoninianus, LEG IIII FLA, centaur with spear right, index mark /C/ , RIC 273, British Museum.

13. Antoninianus, HIR...... , Capricorn left, index mark XXX, RIC - , private collection.

14. Antoninianus, LEG VIIL AVG, bull right, index mark XXIXI, RIC - , found at Ashley Camp, Hants, Winchester Museum.

14a. Antoninianus, LEG VII CL (AVG), bull right, index mark CXXI, RIC 274, British Museum.

14b. 'Denarius', LEG IIII (FL), centaur left with large club, index mark C, RIC 187, British Museum.

15-16. CARAUSIUS, antoninianus, obv. IMPCARAVSIVSPFAVG, rev. CON COC, female with sceptre at altar (or in front of Pharos ?), no index mark,
2.46 gms., 19 mm., RIC - , private collection.

17-18. CARAUSIUS, antoninianus, as above, 3.11 gms., 20 mm., RIC - , private collection.

19-20. CARAUSIUS, antoninianus, obv. IMP CARAVSIVSCPFAVG, rev.VICTOR(IA AVG), Victoria stanging left, no index mark ?, 3.37 gms., 21 mm.,RIC - , private collection.

21. CARAUSIUS, antoninianus, obv. IMP CARAVSIVSPFAVG, apparent jugate bust with Tetricus I is caused by overstriking, rev. PAX AVG, Pax standing with vertical sceptre and olive branch, no index mark, 2.25 gms., 20 mm., RIC 880, from Lydney, Glos., National Museum of Wales, Cardiff.

22. QUINTILLUS (for deified Claudius II), antoninianus, obv. DIVO CLAUDIO, overstruck on obverse of Claudius II, rev. CONSECRATIO, large altar, 2.79 gms, 22 mm., RIC 261, private collection.

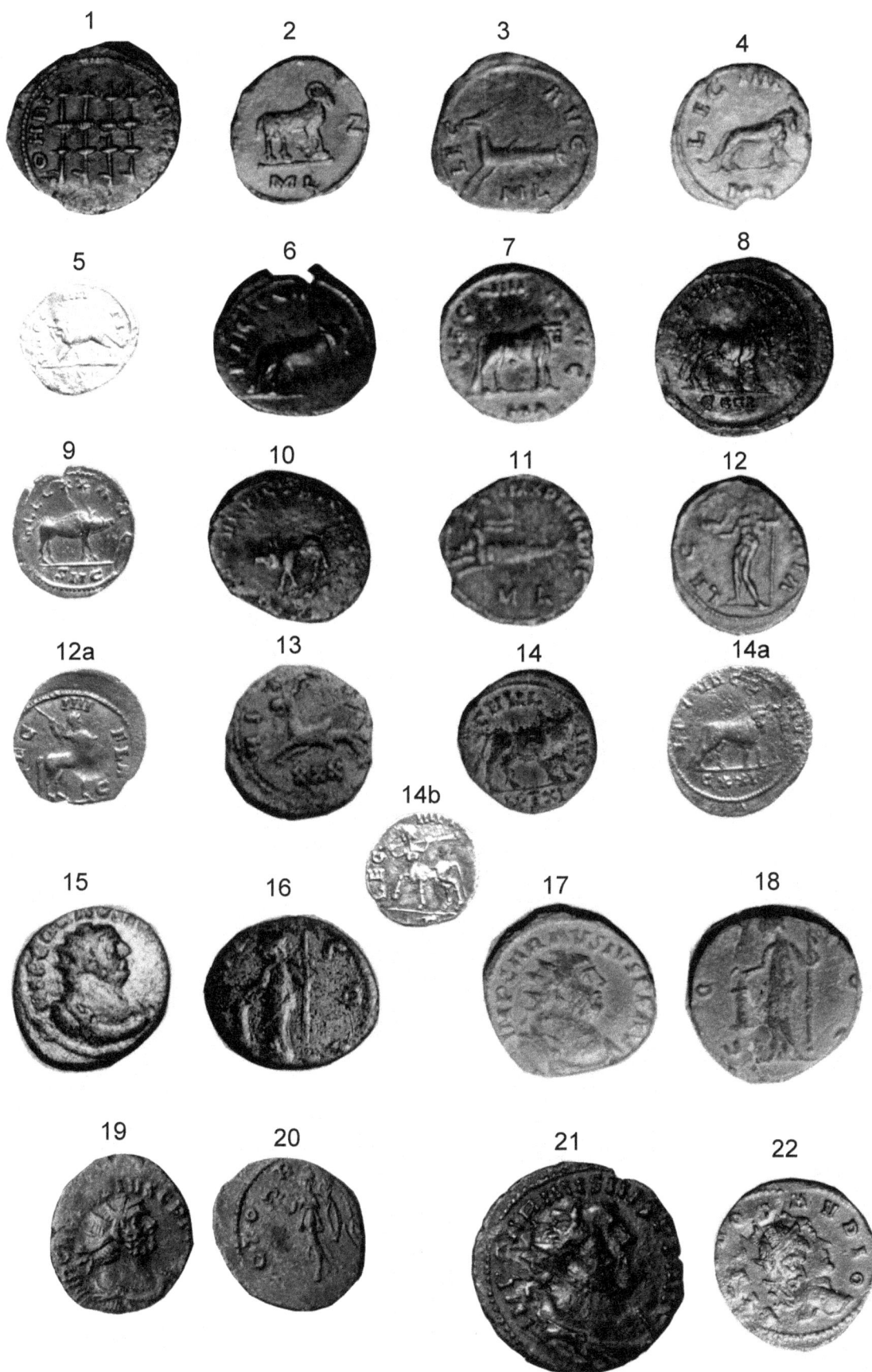

1

2

3

4

5

6

7

8

9

10

11

12

12a

13

14

14a

14b

15

16

17

18

19

20

21

22

Plate 5

Plate 6

1-2. CARAUSIUS, antoninianus, obv. IMPCARAVSIVSPFAVG, rev. FORT REDVX, Fortuna standing left, no index mark, 3.62 gms., 23 mm., RIC - ,
'1987' Hoard, private collection.

3-4. CARAUSIUS, antoninianus, obv. IMPC CARAVSIVS PAVG, rev. PAX AVG, Pax with vertical sceptre and olive branch, index mark S/C/ , 4.79 gms., 23 mm., RIC 476, '1987' Hoard, private collection.

5-6. CARAUSIUS, antoninianus, obv. IMPC CARAVSIVSPFAVG, rev. SAECVLVM FEL, emperor? standing right holding globe and spear, index
mark S/C/ , RIC - , '1987' Hoard, private collection.

7-8. CARAUSIUS, antoninianus, obv. VIRTUS CARAVSI, helmeted bust left, rev. COMES (AVG), Victory standing left, index mark C, RIC - , '1987'
Hoard, private collection.

9-10. CARAUSIUS, antoninianus, obv. IMP CARAVSIVSPFAVG, rev. PAX AVG, Pax holding cornucopia and large branch, no index mark, RIC 909(var.),Verulamium Museum, St. Albans.

11-12. CARAUSIUS, antoninianus, obv. IMPCARAVSIVSPFAVG, rev. TVTELA AVG, Tutela standing left at altar, no index mark, 3.50 gms., 20mm., RIC - , private collection. (This is a product of a British mint).

13-14. CARAUSIUS, antoninianus, obv. IMP CARAVSIVSPFAV, rev. SECA....,Securitas standing left resting on pillar, arm aloft , index mark + x, 2.85 gms.,20 mm., RIC -, private collection.

15-16. CARAUSIUS, copper laureatte, obv. IMP CARAVSIVSPFAV, rev. SECVRITPERPET, type as above, index mark xx , 19 mm., RIC - , private collection.

17-18. ALLECTUS, antoninianus, obv. IMPC ALLECTVSPFAVG, rev. PROVIDENTIA AVG, Providentia standing left with transverse sceptre and
globe, index mark S/P/CL, 3.89 gms., 23 mm, RIC 105, private collection.

19. CARAUSIUS, DIOCLETIAN and MAXIMIAN, antoninianus obv: IMPP CAESS PII PF FR AVGGG, jugate busts of Carausius, Diocletian and Maximian   Rev: PAX AVGGG, Pax standing with transverse sceptre and olive branch, index mark S/P/MLXXI 4.08gms.

Plate 6

Plate 7

1. CARAUSIUS, antoninianus, obv. IMPCARAVSIVS PFAVG, rev. LEG XX VV, boar standing right, no index mark, 3.74gms, 22mm, RIC82, Little Orme's Head   Hoard I, British Museum.

2-3. CARAUSIUS, antoninianus, obv. IMP CARAVSIVS PFAVG, rev.COS(....)III, Emperor standing left holding globe, no index mark, 20mm., RIC - , found at Chalgrove, Oxon., Ashmolean Museum.

4-5. CARAUSIUS, antoninianus, as above but CO(........)L III, 3.43gms, 20 mm., RIC - , private collection.

6-7. CARAUSIUS, aureus, obv. IMPC CARAVSIVSPFAVG consular? bust left, rev. CONCORDIA MILIT, index mark VM, 3.61 gms.(pierced), 20 mm.,RIC 623, Bibliothèque Nationale, Paris.

8-9. CARAUSIUS, antoninianus, obv. IMP CARAVSIVSPAVG, rev.PMTRPIIIICPP, emperor standing left holding globe, index mark C, 4.41 gms.,
 23mm., RIC - , '1987' Hoard, private collection.

10-11. CARAUSIUS, antoninianus, obv. IMP CARAVSIVSPFAVG, rev. PMT(RPV)COSPP ? emperor seated left, index mark MC, 4.34 gms, 23 mm.,
RIC - , '1987' Hoard, private collection.

12-13. CARAUSIUS, antoninianus, obv. IMP CARAVSIVSPAVG, rev. RESTIT BRITAN Carausius raising Britannia, index mark C, 4.54 gms, 25 mm., RIC - , '1987' Hoard, Private collection.

14-15. CARAUSIUS, antoninianus, obv. VIRTVS CARAVSI, armed bust left, rev. MONETA AVG, index mark unclear, 19 mm., RIC 863, Little Orme's Head Hoard I, British Museum.

16. CARAUSIUS, antoninianus, obv. IMP CARAVSIVSPFAVG, rev. PAX AVG, Pax standing with vertical sceptre and olive branch, index mark unclear, 3.02 gms, 20 mm., RIC 880, private collection. (This photograph is turned through 180° in order to clearly show the undertype of the bust of Tetricus I.)

17. CARAUSIUS. antoninianus. Obv: IMP CARAVSIVS PF AVG, bust right Rev:SAECVLARES AVG, cippus inscribed COS IIII. British Museum

18. CARAUSIUS. antoninianus. Obv: IMP CARAVSIVS PF AVG, bust right Rev: PRIET C, horned and bearded god standing right, holding baton and two-footed staff, + in field above. RIC- 21mm. 4.60gms. private collection

19. . CARAUSIUS. antoninianus. Obv: IMP CARAVSIVS PF AVG, bust right Rev: ….. VV, Herculean figure holding whip, walking left, cloak flying behind, + in field left RIC -. 22mm. 5,83gms. Private collection

Plate 7

www.ingramcontent.com/pod-product-compliance
Lightning Source LLC
Chambersburg PA
CBHW061009030426
42334CB00033B/3415